AND GOD REMEMBERED NOAH:

A MOTHER'S HEART-OPENING JOURNEY THROUGH 22 WEEKS IN THE NICU

Naomi D. Williams

Printed in the United States of America

First Printing, 2018

ISBN-13: 978-1985863057
ISBN-10: 1985863057

Naomi D. Williams
PO Box 1262
Evans, GA 30809

www.NaomiDWilliams.com

Forward

"Hold her up to the window so we can see her." Hold her, how I wished I could hold her. A friend came to the NICU to visit and asked that I hold my daughter up to the window; my friend wanted to see her. She was thinking of a newborn nursery where healthy babies are wrapped in pink blankets and bundled into bassinets. There are no windows here, I told her. My daughter was on a heart-lung bypass machine called ECMO. Marilyn was medically paralyzed to prevent her from moving. Her blood was being removed from her body and returned through a complicated web of tubes and filters. I couldn't hold her that day, or the next. I did hold her, once. She was forty-two days old, as old as she would ever be.

My NICU journey began on December 28, 1993. My daughter, Marilyn, was born with a diaphragmatic hernia. She died just before Valentine's day in 1994. It has been 23 years since my NICU journey began. My life has weaved and wandered in directions that would have been incomprehensible to me when I was sitting next to Marilyn's NICU bed. In those difficult days, I lived hour by hour. My days were ruled by numbers on a monitor and winces of pain on my daughter's face. Nothing had gone as planned. In my naivety, I assumed all babies are born bright and rosy and full of life. I imagined my most difficult problems would be colic or figuring out how to pay for college. My NICU experience forever changed how I see the world. Since 1999 I have worked in a level IV NICU. I am a NICU nutritionist, a pediatric nutrition specialist, and am currently pursuing a PhD. Over the years, Naomi and I have formed a very unique and special friendship. Since Marilyn's death I have had two healthy sons, Robbie and Sawyer. My youngest son, Sawyer, is Noah's age. I had just returned from maternity leave when I first met Noah. He was my patient in the NICU. I wrote his feeding plans and monitored his growth. I remember his chubby face and sweet smile. He was the darling of the NICU. I also remember his mom, she was a feisty one. She advocated and fought for her baby unlike any mother I had seen before. Naomi would never settle for the first answer she was given. She demanded more, she demanded answers! When the answers didn't sit well with her, she demanded explanation. She fought to be included in decision making. She fought for Noah. I liked her immensely.

Though our NICU paths took very different directions, Naomi and I share a unique experience. We have served as missionaries together, we worship together, and we have sons the same age. I turned the pain of my daughter's death into a career spent helping fragile infants grow and thrive. Naomi has turned Noah's experience into a lifelong mission of celebrating the differently abled child. God is amazing like that; tears become rivers of life, confusion becomes clarity and hurt becomes triumph.
In And God Remembered Noah, Naomi shares her day to day NICU experience. Through her insightful and heartfelt journal, we follow Noah as he traverses the complexity of extreme prematurity, seizures, feeding tubes, and surgeries. We celebrate Noah's small victories and feel Naomi's pain when she finally realizes how difficult Noah's journey will be. As I read, I feel the anger that has been dormant inside my own heart for 23 years begin to rise. I can't help but feel her fury, her disappointment, and ultimately her joy.

If you're a parent just beginning your NICU journey, you need to read this book. You will find comfort in Naomi's bluntness and humor. Noah's journey will inspire you to put one foot in front of the other, to cry when you need to, and to fight for your little fighter. In the middle of your NICU experience, you will find it hard to imagine what the future will hold for your baby. I wish I could give you the answers you're searching for, but you know I can't. I can reassure you that wherever that path takes you and your baby, God is with you. As you read this book, you will feel God's presence as he comforted Noah and gave strength to Naomi. I encourage you to read the Bible verses Naomi has carefully selected for each entry. As you navigate the ups and downs that are to come, look to the One who created your baby for direction.

If someone you love has a NICU baby, read this book. There are no windows in the NICU. There are tubes, wires, monitors, ventilators and a host of other realities no infant should have to endure. Naomi's book will help you to understand the range of emotions NICU families go through. Before you open your mouth to provide comfort or advice, first you must try to understand the NICU world. NICU parents are hurting; they are also excited about poop. Read this book, and you will know why it's important for you to be excited about poop, too.
For my fellow NICU clinicians, read this book. If you're new to the NICU, welcome, it's a crazy place. You might be an entry in a parent's journal today. Whether you realize it or not, you are part of a family's journey. Long after the baby has been discharged, the care you provided will be remembered. Your tone, your smile, and your sincerity will help a mother get through the most challenging day of her life. Your kind words and honesty will help her make the most difficult decision she will ever have to make. Reading this book will help you to understand why parents fixate on the things they do. Naomi will help you to understand why that baby's mom is so angry! When she is angry, listen to her anger. Try to see the NICU from the perspective of the baby and the mom. Read And God Remembered Noah, and you will see your job from an entirely different perspective.

"My presence will go with you, and I will give you rest." Exodus 33:14
Amy Gates, RD, CSP, LD
NICU Mom, Neonatal Dietitian, Pediatric Nutrition Specialist, Missionary

Table of Contents

Introduction

"How's Noah doing?"

This simple question prompted the pages you're about to read. This is a book about the 22 weeks my premature son Noah spent in the NICU.

This book started out as a journal of our roller coaster ride on a website called Caring Bridge. I found myself retelling the story of each day in the NICU over and over, and realizing I was leaving out important details. Sometimes, by the end of the day, I'd be too tired to share any updates. By journaling our experience online, I was able to share every day (and sometimes twice a day) experiences with all of our friends and family. We could all join in on the collective prayers, making our voice stronger. Capturing and releasing the ups and downs of the day was my therapy. I needed these entries as much as my family and friends who were anxious for updates.

Initially, I wrote these words for Noah.

While writing them, I imagined reading each journal entry to him when he was older. I never imagined I'd share these journal entries with the world. However, as the NICU roller coaster ride finally ended we immediately hopped onto the next roller coaster ride called life. The NICU experience and life after the NICU taught me how to redefine success and how to live my best life, and I want to share this with you.

I didn't start keeping the web-based journal on the Caring Bridge website until Noah was five weeks old. I had tangible paper journals that I would write in here and there, but with motherhood, I have no idea where these are now. His delivery and the first four weeks of Noah's life are a summary of what I remember and what others recounted to me.

On paper, my child is a train wreck, and by medical standards, he doesn't have "quality of life." I'm here to share that Noah has an amazing life today. We just celebrated his eighth birthday. It's not an easy life for either of us, yet we live out loud, are comfortable with the uncomfortable and do everything that we want and can afford to do. We've learned to adapt to this differently-abled ride called disability.

Each chapter covers in detail what was happening each week, medically with Noah, emotionally with me, and lists specific prayer requests. These reflect the ups and downs and often dramatic shift of events. The timeline and sequence of events I describe in these chapters might be flip flopped as time eludes me.

I'm perfectly imperfect, and I'm finally good with that. This book is my truth and one of the hardest things I've done. In these pages, I'm exposing myself, my thoughts, and my fears.

Silliness is one of my coping mechanisms. In difficult times my emotions run high. Being able to laugh helps me handle sticky situations. This means you might read some seemingly crass or inappropriate jokes—I get it from my mom.

I'm not a sailor, but sometimes I have a potty mouth. There were times along this journey when I used four letter words, and those words aren't "love", but I say them with love. I've cleaned it up a little in these pages so my son won't learn this from me.

If you take nothing else away from this book, please become an advocate, and understand what advocacy is. Learn how to become an efficient and effective advocate for you, your child, and your family.

If you're a parent who finds yourself in the NICU, I hope you find comfort in these pages knowing you are not alone. If you're a medical professional, I invite you to experience the NICU from a different perspective. If you have a loved one who is traveling this tricky road through the NICU right now, I hope this book helps you offer your support where it's needed most.

As you read these words, I hope you feel enlightened, educated, and empowered.

Will you join me aboard this very real roller coaster ride?

"Our deepest fear is not that we are inadequate. Our deepest fear is that we are powerful beyond measure. It is our light not our darkness that most frightens us. We ask ourselves, who am I to be brilliant, gorgeous, talented and fabulous? Actually, who are you not to be? You are a child of God. Your playing small does not serve the world. There's nothing enlightened about shrinking so that other people won't feel insecure around you.

We were born to make manifest the glory of God that is within us. It's not just in some of us; it's in everyone. And as we let our own light shine, we unconsciously give other people permission to do the same. As we are liberated from our own fear, our presence automatically liberates others." Our Greatest Fear, Marianne Williamson

Let's begin.

"Every living thing on the face of the earth was wiped out... Only Noah was left and those with him in the ark. The waters flooded the earth one hundred and fifty days. But God remembered Noah..." (Genesis 7:23-8:1)

Please keep in mind that I am not a medical professional and the words in this book are not medical advice. I'm also using some alias names to protect people. At the end of this book, you'll find a glossary containing explanations of the terms that may have left you scratching your head. These are here to make reading this book a little easier for you.

Pregnancy
The best thing at the worst time

My pregnancy was the best thing, but it came at the worst time, and a pivotal time in my life. Looking back, it ultimately helped me revive my dreams and realign my priorities. I was in a disheveled transition. In an attempt to end my messy transitional time, I was in the process of going into the military. My plans were slightly stifled because I didn't meet the weight or tape requirements to enlist. I had already planned a trip to California, which gave me the time and incentive to work on losing the weight. My recruiter said, "There are three things that can't happen before you go: You can't have any new piercings, you can't have any new tattoos, and you can't be pregnant." My response, "Okay, cool. Not a problem."

Off to California, I went—for a month.

There's only one Virgin Mary

When I learned I was pregnant, 1 thought, holy shit, how'd this happen? Considering there's only one virgin

Mary, my kiddo was conceived the old fashioned way. I was in total denial this was happening. I was late, but I figured it was stress. To take away all doubt I bought a one-dollar pregnancy test. To my surprise, it was positive—it had to be a false positive. I visited another store and bought a two-pack test. To my dismay and chagrin, both of those tests had a positive reading. To be absolutely sure, my next step was to visit the health department and have a blood test. All of these pee tests could be false positives—my blood won't lie.

I couldn't get an appointment before I left California, so I traveled home believing I could be pregnant. I made it back to Georgia and had a blood test which confirmed all the pee tests were right. I met with my recruiter and said, "Well, my time in California wasn't as productive as I would have liked. I didn't get any tattoos or piercings, I didn't lose weight, but I did learn I gained a person." He looked confused for a minute but finally put things together. That was the end of my military career. This was definitely unplanned.

Before getting knocked up, I had been laid off from my grant-funded job. I had just finished my master's program, and I was unable to secure anything that would support me, hence my job search and excursion to California. In an attempt to be a responsible adult I rented out my home, so I didn't risk going into foreclosure, and moved in with my dad.

In the beginning, I was totally embarrassed about my pregnancy. I wasn't married and I wasn't publicly dating, so this was out of character and hard to explain. To say I shocked many in my family and my immediate circle is an understatement. Several people were upset and disappointed, and others were overjoyed that I was finally going to be a mom. I was still in transition, as things didn't pan out in California, so it was imperative to start putting things in place to support this new person I was growing inside of me.

A natural plan

You probably have some questions right now about Noah's dad. We had been friends for many years. By all accounts, he was my "person," you know, just like Meredith and Cristina on Grey's Anatomy. The last weekend we were together I decided we wanted different things and that we'd be better off as friends. He wasn't married; he just didn't want a child. He didn't live nearby either, drastically limiting his physical presence pre and post delivery. I knew our relationship would be tested, yet I wasn't prepared for the abandonment and fallout that was about to happen.

I knew I wanted to at least attempt a natural birth, but the midwife I wanted to work with was no longer practicing in my area. I considered going to her anyway but decided it would be risky when going into labor and getting to her 90 minutes away. I chose a local midwife who would respect my decisions and help me through the birthing process when things got hard.

I found a childbirth educator who focused on the Bradley method, worked out of her home, and lived way out in the country. At my first visit, she explained what we'd be doing, how each session would progress, and had me detail what I wanted and how I envisioned my birthing experience. To give a brief sense of the pain I might experience, she had me lie down on the couch and asked me to open my hand. The lights were dimmed, and I recall the smell of a soothing essential oil filling the air. She took a piece of ice and had me hold it on my fingertips. I was to let her know when the sensation was too intense and I could no longer take it. I remember withstanding the discomfort longer than any of us anticipated. The whole point of the exercise was to begin teaching me that there would be times of pain and intense discomfort yet my body was built to do this, and my mind was the biggest obstacle. I could control my experience with breathing, meditation, and my support system. From that moment I determined who would and wouldn't be in my delivery room. Not everyone supported or understood my desire for a natural birth, and I wasn't about to have any negativity blowing up my zen.

A mostly smooth ride

My pregnancy didn't come at my ideal time in life, yet I was determined to make it the best experience possible. My first trimester was great. At eight weeks I had both boy and girl names picked out. The name would be either Noah which means comfort or Hannah which means grace. I didn't have any kind of morning sickness, and I didn't have any weird cravings. McDonald's was definitely something Noah didn't like, yet he thoroughly enjoyed the "eat more chickin" place (Chick-fil-A).

Initially, I thought I was going to have a girl, so I had to adjust my thinking when I found out I was having a boy. I was a bit intimidated on how I'd raise a boy not knowing anything about boys. As time went on, I got excited about having a boy and enjoyed mentally planning all the wonderful and gross things we'd get into. Boys are rare in my family so I knew we'd be celebrating!

When I started the second trimester my body started acting a bit funny. I lacked energy, my feet started to swell, and my blood pressure was beginning to creep up. In hindsight, I should have spoken up sooner when my pressure was outside of my "normal" range.

There are some childhood habits I never grew out of and checking my blood pressure was one of them. My dad had blood pressure issues, so he had monitors at his house. Even before I was preggo, when I'd go to his house, I would "play" with his blood pressure machine and check my pressure. I continued this habit while pregnant.

Concerns are inching up

Over time I noticed my blood pressure going from being around 117 to 125 to 130. As my pressure was creeping up, I noticed my feet started swelling. One particular day, my go-to, wide, most comfortable shoes that I wore all the time were hurting and cutting off my circulation. I finished work, got home and checked my blood pressure, and it was 150/100. This prompted my first concerned phone call to the midwife's office. I'm not a doctor, yet I knew this wasn't a normal blood pressure since I used to work with women who fell into a high-risk pregnancy category. We worked to address factors that could cause bad outcomes for a mother or her baby. I'm telling you this to show you that my education and work experience also contributed to me knowing the symptoms and that the blood pressure I was experiencing were cause for concern.

When I called the midwife's office, they told me that if I felt I needed to go to the ER, then I should do so. WHAT?! I don't remember if I went to the hospital then or not. I had just gotten to the point where I was looking for another OB/GYN as a backup in the event I needed medical intervention. Although my midwife was in a practice with OB/GYNs, I wasn't a fan of two of the doctors there, and didn't know enough about the third physician partner, making me uncomfortable to go under their care should my pregnancy turn high-risk.

My blood pressure prompted a couple more calls and visits to the hospital. Late one night, my mom took me to the ER because my pressure was hanging out around 190/100 and not coming down. I was put into a room on the labor and delivery floor for observation, and while being monitored, my blood pressure stayed in the medical normal range. The nurse returned to the room and shared part of the phone conversation she had with the doctor—they told me I was a hypochondriac because I was monitoring my pressure at home. The nurse said, "We don't normally have moms checking their pressure at home." Swelling and elevated blood pressure were the only two preeclamptic pregnancy symptoms I had. Because I didn't have any other issues and wasn't complaining about headaches or seeing spots, the hospital sent me home and told me to follow-up with my midwife.

Happy Birthday—here's some bedrest

Around June 6, 2009, and around 24 weeks pregnant, I was put on bedrest and started taking blood pressure medicine. Over the next week, I had my glucose test and had the pleasure of doing a 24-hour urine collection—collecting urine for a full 24 hours in a big ugly red container, which needed to stay cool until I returned it to the lab. It's to test kidney function. The urine is checked for protein, and if they detect higher amounts of protein (protein spilling), it's often a sign of kidney damage or disease.

I had to spend my birthday inside, yet my friends made turning 32 special as they came to me and we had a game night at my mom's house.

Being on bedrest was an interesting ordeal. The nurse told me I couldn't watch TV, couldn't go anywhere except to the bathroom, and my room had to be dark and quiet. My first thought was, what year is this again?

I came to find out I didn't require the strict bedrest the nurse suggested; she was upset I woke her up (insert crazy shocked face emoji). I came off bedrest on a Friday, went back to work that weekend, and received a call on Monday morning from the midwife telling me to go back on bedrest—something wasn't quite right with my blood work.

By this point, I had just hit the 15-pound weight gain mark. I was too big to fit into my usual clothes, not quite big enough to fill out maternity clothes, and I had a little noticeable bump.

Something isn't right

Tuesday evening I went to church—I didn't drive, and I stayed seated. I was feeling a bit weak, so I had a friend take me home early. Although I had been eating throughout the day, I hadn't felt Noah move. My blood pressure was fine, so I opted not to call the midwife's office as I didn't want to be ridiculed by the staff again. On Wednesday morning when I got up, I still didn't feel any movement. I drank some orange juice (Noah's favorite) and still no movement. I had my mom take me to the ER as I knew this didn't feel right and I left a message at the midwife's office telling them I was on my way.

When I got to the labor and delivery floor, they hooked me up to some monitors. The nurse caring for me was nice, but her words were awful. She said, "Aww you're just a paranoid first-time mom. Everything will be fine."

I was hooked up to monitors so they could check for movement. They bring me 16-20 ounces of juice, I take it, and there's still no movement. They brought me some more juice about 30 minutes later, with the same result—NO MOVEMENT. The staff said they were call-

ing and leaving messages for my doctor and waiting for a
call back. Sometime late morning the midwife called my
cell phone, and we had an interesting (hindsight disturb-
ing) exchange.

Me: "You got my message. I've had a lot of juice, and he's
still not moving. They're monitoring me."
Midwife: "Oh, you're already at the hospital? That's why
I was calling, telling you to go." (There was protein in my
urine, and my kidney levels were off.)
Me: "You didn't get my message? I called and left it with
the answering service." Midwife: "No, I haven't gotten
anything."

The nurse returns and tells me that my doctor is out of
town which is why they weren't getting a return call. We
then work to get on the same page as I remind them I
see the midwife in that office, not a physician.

Today was supposed to be my next childbirth education
session. I called my childbirth educator and let her know
that I wouldn't be able to make our appointment. She
was a bit shocked that I took the time to call her to can-
cel. I hoped to reschedule and would let her know once I
was released.

Lunch time rolled around; I was getting super hungry
as all I've had is a bunch of juice. My other dad (stepdad
Louis) went to get me a fish sandwich to satisfy a huge
craving for something salty and substantial. The hospital
staff discussed getting me a catheter, but they tabled this
discussion for now. Fortunately, yet unfortunately, they
changed their minds.

Releasing my bladder while not being over a toilet felt mind-altering and embarrassing. Louis came back with lunch, and the room smelled heavenly. Fried fish sandwich, French fries, cole slaw—oh, that was about to be my life! Then the nurse comes in and tells me I can't eat. It was a precaution just in case I needed to be transferred to another hospital. The practice that my midwife belonged to had delivering privileges at two hospitals in our area. This particular hospital had a pseudo intensive care unit for babies, but it wasn't robust enough to handle a baby as immature as Noah would be if delivered that day.

The midwife came to see me and said she was going to transfer my care to an MFM (maternal fetal medicine) doctor—a subspecialist who works with high-risk pregnant women. Oh boy, I was becoming one of the high-risk women I used to work with.

This wasn't the direction I wanted to go, but I knew I'd be in much better hands and under better care in the event something bad happened. I just wasn't ready for it to be today.

The midwife was arranging for me to be transported by ambulance to the other hospital, I was still being monitored, and it seemed Noah had a strong heartbeat—I often wondered if we were listening to mine and not his. The nurse came in to check me and had a concerned look on her face. When I asked her about it, I don't remember getting an answer. When she had the look on her face again, I looked at the monitor print out and started asking more questions. Noah started having activity, but it wasn't the good kind.

After six hours of monitoring and no movement, the monitor noted two decelerations; instead of the lines going up with movement, the lines went down meaning he was having trouble.

The Delivery
God breathes on Noah for the second time

The EMS team arrived to take me to the other hospital. As I lay on the stretcher in front of the nurses' station waiting on my transfer chart, one of the partner physicians walked into the unit. I thought he was coming to see me, but he wasn't. He had no idea who I was and why I was talking to him—facial expressions don't lie.

My mom wasn't able to ride with me, so the ambulance waited for her to get her car and follow us to the other hospital 15 minutes away. They didn't consider my transfer an emergency, so there was no need for the drama of speeding and sirens.

When we arrived at the hospital, we entered through the ER and headed to the labor and delivery floor. While en route, the transport team stopped and casually chatted with another EMS team in the hallway before I finally landed in a room and moved to a bed.

ALL. HELL. BREAKS. LOOSE.

A frantic medical team enters the room, and they promptly worked to get a good blood pressure reading for Noah and me. The staff ushered my mom into the corner and cut off my brand new bra and white maternity pants (my feelings were very hurt about that).

The hospital staff waited impatiently for the ultrasound machine, and it confirmed their fear. I don't know for certain what the ultrasound showed, and I don't know exactly what they were afraid of, but I knew it wasn't good and that my kiddo must have been in trouble. As soon as the ultrasound confirmed the team's thoughts, I was rushed down the hall to the operating room to have an emergency c-section—I was in the hospital room all of 10 minutes.

My mother was left standing in the room in a daze, and the last thing I remember hearing after they wheeled me into the operating room was the doctor and anesthesiologist arguing about my blood pressure.

"If you don't put her to sleep we are going to lose the baby."

...

"I don't know what her blood pressure is, and it's not safe to put her under."

At 3:45 pm on June 17, 2009, Noah Samuel entered this world at 26 weeks, 1 pound, 10 ounces, just over a foot long, and lifeless. His APGAR scores were 0,0,0 at one minute and 1,0,0 at five minutes. APGAR is a score given to quickly summarize a newborn's health. It stands for Appearance, Pulse, Grimace, Activity, and Respiration (heart rate, respiration and muscle tone are three primary components they look at). It took five minutes and shots of epinephrine to revive him (I learned this later on in our hospital stay).

God breathed on Noah and has been keeping him ever since

Noah was born at 26 weeks gestation; three and a half months premature. His umbilical cord was wrapped around his neck, and it was "dead" so there was no blood flow, and he measured what they would expect to see if I were 20 weeks pregnant resulting in IUGR (intrauterine growth restriction) which made Noah smaller than he should have been for his gestational age. The neonatologist that delivered him was livid saying he was tired of delivering "crack" babies. For the record, I've never used drugs. The condition Noah was in was unfathomable and dismal. My mother shared with the doctor that I wasn't a drug user and that I did everything that I knew to take care of myself to have a good pregnancy and ultimately a healthy baby.

Waking up to a dark room and an unexpected gift

The last thing I remembered was hearing the high-risk doctor and anesthesiologist arguing about my blood pressure, and then semi-waking up to a dark room full of family and someone holding a Polaroid picture of a tiny person connected to and covered with wires and tubes. That was my first introduction to my son. He was considered a micro preemie. The nurse who brought the picture knew from personal experience what it was like to have a micro preemie and not be able to see, touch or hold them right after delivery, and she never wanted another mother to experience that feeling. She brought this picture of Noah to me since I couldn't get to him. That was the first of many intangible gifts I received along our NICU journey. I remember seeing the picture and hearing people talk about Noah but being unable to process the conversations and then going back to sleep. It was 48 hours before I actually saw him in person.

Two days after I delivered Noah, my mom wheeled me down to the NICU to see Noah for the first time. It's a good thing I was already sitting.

Weeks 1-4
Perfectly and wonderfully made

Noah Samuel, God broke the mold when he made you and knew you before you were formed in my womb. You are perfectly and wonderfully made. You have endured more than most have in a lifetime. You have brought me into a different, privileged, and beautiful world. You are my hero, and I am proud to be your mom. I love you with my life, and I truly celebrate not just your "born-day," but your life. It's not an easy life, but we're making it the best life. I cherish every day we have together.

We sat in front of double-sided automatic doors, but you have to get permission from the "voice" behind the doors before you're allowed in. It's like the scene from The Wizard of Oz when Dorothy has the exchange with the all powerful wizard. Ours was without all the smoke, bells, and whistles. Once we had permission, we had to stop at the trough sink and wash our hands for three minutes. It was difficult for me to stand and uncomfortable to bend over and in the sink to get to the water but

I did what I had to do. You have to wash to your elbows regardless if you'll be holding a baby or not—it's a precaution to eliminate germs and infection.

After I washed my hands, I stopped by the unit desk to find out where I could find my baby. This NICU was set up with six separate rooms that could hold up to eight babies each. Noah had taken up residence in the first room on the right.

Stably unstable

Man, seeing that little boy was a sight for sore eyes. It was challenging and breathtaking to see this little person, who could fit in the palm of my hand, connected and covered with so many tubes and wires. I cried—tears of joy that he had made it, tears of fear as I knew what his early arrival could mean and the outcomes that we might have, then, tears of pain because my stomach had been cut open and I was still very sore. I sat and looked at him for what seemed like hours even though it was just minutes.

I got an update on his stability—which was really more of an update on what was stable as he was in such an unstable state. They actually didn't expect him to live hours let alone make it for several days. I went back to my room to rest. Noah was very, very sick and spent all of his energy fighting for his life in these early, very critical days. He was so fragile. Another NICU mom later told me that she used to feel so scared just sitting next to him and used to cry just looking at his teeny body.

I was ill, really ill

I didn't realize how sick I really was until a couple of weeks after I delivered. It's typical for a woman to stay in the hospital a day or two after having a c-section. I was so sick that I stayed a week. They put me on magnesium sulfate which made me very hot and turned everyone else into popsicles because I required the air conditioning to be as low as it could go. One morning, I felt extremely weird. It's hard to describe, but I was very anxious, and my heart was beating way too fast. While we waited for the staff to see me and check my blood pressure, I began putting my last will and testament on a cocktail size napkin as I didn't know what was going on or what was going to happen to me. I can laugh at this now, but my mom still doesn't think it was funny.

I was swollen, and my blood pressure was so high; it was at stroke level. I was restarted on a blood pressure medicine to help get it under control, and was on it for a couple of days before I started feeling weird again. Then, I found myself at the other end of the spectrum moving like a pendulum—my blood pressure was too low. I'm a bit fired up and mad at this point. Who's monitoring my care? Why am I having to "catch" all of this?! The response I received was because I had delivered and was

25

technically no longer high-risk I was transferred back to the midwife's office (insert confused and arched eyebrow emoji).

I honestly don't remember if the midwife came to see me within the first couple of days after delivery. I do remember one of the partnering physicians coming to my room; the one I met while transferring from the other hospital. I had a real bad pain in my mouth. He stood at the end of my bed, close to the wall and just listened to me talk. He didn't examine me, he didn't touch me, he didn't do shit other than hold up the wall and nod his head, so I was really confused as to why he came. My theory was to say that he made his rounds—technically he wasn't wrong.

My best friend from college came to visit me from Columbia. She brought with her a beautiful pastel blanket that her mom crocheted for Noah. Although it was for him, I slept with it for several nights. I took her down, well technically, she rolled me down, to see Noah in the NICU. There was a cart full of books provided by the March of Dimes, and we grabbed a few so we could have story time. I read "The Very Hungry Caterpillar" by Eric Carle. We were bewildered how this was a children's book outside of the illustrations. To say we needed a dictionary as we read was an understatement. We laughed so long and so hard about "decoding" that book. For instance, the beginning pages talks about an aphid—what child knows what an aphid is? How many adults can explain what it is? This friend always provided comic relief, and this time was no different.

Going home—alone

I was discharged a week after delivering Noah. The nurse wheeled me down to the hospital entrance, and I sat to the side of the revolving door as I waited for my mom to pull the car around to the front. In my lap, I held, not what I was supposed to be holding—my baby in an infant car seat, yet a plant that was gifted to me along with a mylar balloon that read, "It's a boy!" in blue lettering. As I sat there, I thought, dammit, why didn't I send the balloon with mom when she left to get the car? I didn't want any attention. I didn't want any questions. I didn't want to give any answers or explain where my baby was. As I sat with a waterfall of overwhelming thoughts, a woman gently approached me and just said, "I'll be praying for you and your baby."

About two weeks after having Noah, I saw one of the nurses who took care of him from the time he was born. I hadn't seen her in a few days and was excited to talk with her. I spoke to her as we passed each other in the hall as I went to get Noah a few books from the reading cart. She was cordial, but it wasn't the greeting I was expecting. When I entered Noah's pod and settled in beside his incubator, she realized I was "Noah's mom." She said, "Uh, Naomi I didn't realize that was you when we spoke in the hall. I didn't recognize you!" I told her, "I know, I look different in real clothes versus a house coat. And I'm walking instead of being wheeled in." She responds, "That too, but you were so sick and so swollen. You were in really bad shape. You don't look like the same person." I didn't realize I looked that bad or different, but looking back at pictures I can see just what she was talking about. I was extremely sick.

I eventually learned why I was so sick. I had severe, undiagnosed preeclampsia and I had developed what's known as HELLP syndrome. Remember when I mentioned having to do the 24-hour urine collection? I later learned that it's a screening tool for preeclampsia and HELLP syndrome in pregnancy. When the midwife called on "D-day" (delivery day) to tell me my labs came back with concerns and that I had protein in my urine—this was an indication, and proof that I had preeclampsia.

After I had been discharged from the hospital I had to follow up with the midwife's office to get released from their care. What followed was a challenging conversation. There was no admission of any wrongdoing, yet when I listened to what was said, I knew (and it confirmed) that there were royal fuck-ups with my care. When I went for my six-week check-up with the high-risk doctor (not the midwife), I learned that at the time of delivery I had HELLP syndrome (H-hemolysis, EL- elevated liver enzymes, LP- low platelets) and that my kidneys had begun shutting down. HELLP is a life-threatening complication of pregnancy and is connected with preeclampsia.

As an aside, approximately three years after I had Noah, a friend and former high school classmate living in a different city, had developed preeclampsia and HELLP in her third trimester. Her pregnancy had been on track and had no unusual problems until one day there were. She delivered her baby roughly six weeks early, and by all circumstances, he should have been okay. He lived less than 24 hours. Her blood pressure was out of control. She lost her vision, had seizures, had several mini-strokes and her care team fought hard to save her life. She has since made a full recovery (medically), yet the scars of that life-changing experience are with her forever.

Fighting with every fiber

The fact that I was so sick meant Noah was **extremely sick.** His body was fighting with every fiber he had to stay alive. In one of the many candid conversations I had with Dr. S, he explained not only the trauma endured pre and during birth, but the work that Noah's body had been doing to hold on as long as he did. He explained that his heart was enlarged and like that of a racehorse who'd been in prime racing condition—this is good for a horse, but not for Noah. He had a thick heart which meant he was working super hard, but working harder than it was supposed to. My memory is fuzzy on this, yet I remember his liver wasn't doing all that it should have been. The function of the liver is to detox and take away waste in the body as well as help make special proteins needed for the blood to clot. This was another cause for concern. Noah was jaundiced for months. He had a beautiful chocolate color to him. My mom was excited that she would have four grandbabies: two caramel and two chocolate. It wasn't until months later, as his complexion began to lighten that we realized his coloring was due to how sick he was and his poor liver function.

I just want to hold my baby

I yearned to hold Noah. Regardless of how tiny he was and how intimidating the ventilator and vast amount of wires were, my palms were itching to feel his skin, and my heart ached to feel his breath against my chest. One night a couple of weeks in, his nurse gave me the greatest gift. It was a relatively "quiet" night in the unit, and the babies in our room were behaving well. She said we couldn't hold each other long, but we could snuggle for just a few minutes. I placed the rocking chair next to the incubator, just shy of touching. I removed my shirt so we could kangaroo hold (skin-to-skin). The nurse and respiratory therapist wrapped Noah up like a little burrito and oh so delicately placed him on my chest. Oh, the joy I felt and the wave of emotions that came. We read "Do I Look Good In Color?" then said a prayer and he went back in his incubator.

Don't waste the liquid gold!

I was pumping all of the time—every three hours to ensure I kept my milk supply. I was adamant about breast-feeding; I couldn't put him to breast, so I was determined to pump and make sure he got mommy milk. I learned a hard and hurtful lesson during this time. After pumping, I'd transfer the milk into freezer-safe milk bags. When I finally got the word to start bringing milk in for Noah, I was elated only to get deflated. I had a bag with 4-6 ounces of milk, and at the time he was only going to get 10 ml. So they defrosted my bag of milk and pulled what they could use in the next 24 hours (no more than 30 ml.) and dumped the rest. I was beyond hurt to see all of that "liquid gold" go down the drain.

From that point on, I learned to ration my milk over several bags. The staff wasn't so happy when I'd bring in ten 10 ml. bags of milk when he got up to 30 ml. a feeding, but I was determined to not lose my hard work down the drain again.

A couple of things I learned from pumping that are well worth passing on:

1. You can buy different sizes of the breast pump cups! The cups that come with the machine are standard and a relatively good guess. Yet if your boobs are bigger, you won't get as much milk as you could and it can be painful. If needed you can go with a smaller cup as well—I learned this from another mom.

2. Breast stimulation keeps the milk coming. When your baby is in the NICU, and you can't nurse, you get creative.

My new hangout

I wasn't able to drive so I'd spend the majority of the day at the hospital. A typical day was getting dropped off after 9:00 am and hanging around until 1:00 pm or 4:00 pm and returning after shift change. I would read, sing, and talk with Noah, or just sit and watch him, groveling for the opportunity to hold him. Spending so much time at the hospital, I made friends with the other NICU moms. I made forever friends and lasting connections with Jenny, Indy's mom, and Robin, Emmaline's mom. They made the NICU and the beginning of life outside of it much more bearable. There were twins in the same room named Noah and Samuel—what were the chances? They had a relatively short stay, so I didn't really get to know them or their parents, yet I sure did celebrate with them when they left.

Throughout our stay, we met several other families that had to get used to the idea of having a micro preemie. I remember the baby's name faster than the parents'. Early into our journey, we met baby Phil, his parents, and his grandma. He arrived before Noah and was in a room across the hall. We tended to make connections when several parents are "visiting" at the same time and especially when lining up at the hand washing trough. Through impromptu conversations, you learn the stories, the challenges, and what miracle is needed at that moment. There were also times when I'd never meet the parents but would still say a prayer for them and their little one.

Awakening the determined advocate in me

I had a nurse who continued to silence Noah's monitor. When I asked her why, her response was, "I don't want to wake the bigger babies." She was adamant that Noah was okay and she'd know if he was in distress. Being the person and mom that I am, I watched to see if this was true, and it wasn't. Noah started to bottom out, his monitor was silent, and I had to ask the nurse to come help him. We learned that his monitor was set to be silenced for one minute, and the nurse thought it was set at 30 seconds. Before I left that night, I asked he not have that nurse again for the duration of his stay. I think this was when I became determined to advocate at all costs. I would keep asking questions until I truly understood the answer and became comfortable with his care plan.

I also had a long recovery ahead of me

I had a difficult time recovering from the c-section. They give you a belly pillow to use when changing positions. The idea is to push the pillow into your stomach to bear down on when going to stand or sit. I was a bit jealous when I saw Jenny walk into the unit a couple of days after delivering her twins. Not only was she walking, but walking without a pillow. I wanted to be like her and show this c-section who the boss was. Unfortunately, that didn't happen. I used that pillow for at least three weeks.

It had been three days since I'd eaten and I was finally able to eat again! Remember the fish sandwich my stepdad brought that I wasn't allowed to eat on delivery day? A day or so after delivery when I was conscious enough to ask for food, the staff told me I had to have a bowel movement before I could eat any solids (insert disappointed and heartbroken emoji face). Do you know how hard it is to go when there's nothing solid in your system, and you've been on pain medicines that induce constipation? Fortunately for me and unfortunately for my sister-friend who was with me when I finally had to go. I could make it to the bathroom on my own, but I couldn't get up or get my comfy granny panties up— Perkins to the rescue! This wasn't the job she wanted or signed up for, but she was willing to do whatever was needed to help me. When I finally did get to savor that fish sandwich, it was the best damn fish sandwich I'd ever eaten.

From the time I came home until Noah came home, 1 invaded my mother's space and kept her company every night by sleeping in her bed. I would retreat to my room when Louis was in town, and you guessed it, the day he left, I was back in her bed that night.
What can I say? There's no place like mom's bed. My mom was my rock and support person through this whole ordeal. She had become my "person."

Week 5
Seize the carpe diem

Wednesday, July 22, 2009, 1:32 am, ET

Week 5, Wednesday (morning) prayer requests:
1. *His brain's ability to control and release fluid build-up and his body to absorb it*
2. *Remain infection-free*
3. *Continued good growth*
4. *Clear, mature, and healthy lungs*

This experience is a scenic journey with bends in the road

It's amazing how time is passing by. Five weeks ago today, I was rushed into the OR, and our son was deliv ered; however, it feels like we've been in the hospital for months. I'm thankful for every single prayer sent out and up for Noah's healing and being made whole.

We're grateful for every new day, for this brings us a day closer to being able to take Noah home. No two days are the same, and I'm grateful for that. Each day, we're given a new horizon and sunset, and it's up to us to determine what we see in the middle. Having a micro preemie has definitely enabled me to appreciate the minutest things in life, and lets me see the good in every day and every situation.

When we take a trip, we try to find the shortest route; the one with the least traffic, least resistance, fewest hours, and most efficient on gas. Well, that's the path I would have preferred; however, God knows how much I enjoy His glorious workmanship in nature and has afforded me the opportunity to take the long way. I had been saying that we're taking things day by day, and now, it's moment by moment. We don't have bad days, we have bends in the road; which sometimes turn out to be very sharp curves, but really, it's just a moment in time.

Wednesday, July 22, 2009, 11:50 pm, ET

Week 5, Wednesday (night) prayer requests:
1. *Remain infection-free*
2. *Control cranial fluid*
3. *Lung and body strength to come off the ventilator this week*
4. *Continue good growth*

Seize the day

Today, I started journaling on a website called Caring Bridge as a way to keep everyone up to date and to be able to share our prayer requests with more people.

Noah had a pretty good day today. He weighs a whopping 2 pounds, 14 ounces and is filling out quite nicely. He's doing better with his breathing and is needing less assistance with machine breaths and oxygen. He's still getting my milk, and it's mixed with formula. They've bypassed his stomach, and his milk is going straight to his intestines. This is so he won't have reflux (he was doing very well with his feeding up until this new mixture of breastmilk and formula). His lungs look better than the day before, which is very good—we're hoping to come off of the ventilator this week!

Carpe Diem is the theme for today. Noah had a wonderful first half of the day. When I walked in the room, and the nurse said, "Noah has had a wonderful day," this was music to my ears! We haven't had a "wonderful" day in quite some time. He was so peaceful, his numbers stayed up, and he wasn't setting off the monitors.

I bet you didn't know that babies play the pickup game even at this age. Although Noah and the other preemies can't physically throw anything down, they know how to keep the nurses on their toes. They're all attached to a monitoring system—Noah's system tracks his heart rate, respiration (breaths), and oxygen (O2) saturation. The "game" he plays is he'll drop his O2 levels so it sets the monitor off and the nurse has to turn the O2 up, then he'll wait until they get comfortable in their seats and he'll set the monitor off again by being too high on the O2, so they have to turn it down. Noah isn't the only baby who does this—imagine being in a room with six infants, three of them have monitors going off and the other three are crying simultaneously. I have a great appreciation for the nurses and respiratory therapists who care for Noah and the others.

Today's theme is "Seize the Day" because I missed a perfect opportunity to hold my baby. We normally cuddle in the evening, so I wasn't dressed the way I would have liked to hold him. I figured since he was having such a wonderful day I would just hold him when I came back in the evening. Well, when I returned, my chance had been blown—he had an IV back in his arm giving him antibiotics, and by this time, he had been messed with too much for me to hold him.

It's hard to hold Noah only once a day, and only when he has had a good or relatively non-stressful day. I can't begin to tell you how it feels to have blown the opportunity for us to cuddle. We both benefit and heal when we get to hold each other. I won't make this mistake again.

Noah was resting peacefully tonight. He hasn't been this calm and restful in several days. He wasn't agitated at all; he wasn't trying to pull out any of the tubes. He was just—sleeping. I was comforted knowing that Noah was resting—truly resting when I left tonight. I can rest better when I know he's calm. Many nights when I leave, I'm worried about him having fits. Fits of trying diligently to get the breathing tube out of his mouth and the feeding tube out of his nose. He cries during these fits too, but you can't hear his cries because of the breathing tube. It breaks my heart to see him cry and fight with the tubing because there's absolutely nothing that I can do. Nothing. I feel completely helpless.

Each day is truly a faith walk, and I don't get through each day in my own strength. It's by Christ Jesus that I'm able to maintain and keep it together. The joy of the Lord is my strength, and I remind myself of that daily.

Friday, July 24, 2009, 12:00 am, ET

Week 5, Friday prayer requests:
1. *Stabilize breathing to come off the ventilator*
2. *Remain infection-free*
3. *Control cranial pressure*

When Noah was "small"

Noah has gained an ounce since Wednesday and weighs 2 pounds, 15 ounces now. He had a busy but good day. He had his first eye exam, and it was good, so they'll recheck his eyes again in two weeks. We also received another good report; the cranial ultrasound showed no change in his ventricles—Thank you, Jesus! This means no surgery at this point. *It's common for preemies to develop hydrocephalus—fluid on the brain which often requires a shunt because the brain isn't regulating it properly. The shunt works to keep the fluid from building in the brain.*

I am so proud of Noah. He's becoming more tolerant of people messing with him, which is good—it means his O2 levels aren't dropping as much. He has graduated to a preemie/small diaper and has outgrown his first blood pressure cuff. I find this funny because I catch myself saying, "when he was small…" He's still so small, just not as small as he once was.

Week 6
Conductor,
can we get off this roller coaster?

Wednesday, July 29, 2009, 3:29 pm, ET

Week 6, Wednesday prayer requests:
1. *Maintain heart rate and oxygen saturation within allotted numbers*
2. *Good growth and remain infection-free*

I'm melting-down on this roller coaster ride

Noah is six weeks old today! Overall, he's okay. He weighs 3 pounds, 1 ounce, and is growing well. We've moved from the room he's been in since birth, so we have new roommates. We miss Indy and her parents very much. Emmaline was our roommate in the new room for about a week; however, she went home yesterday—we are so grateful!

So much has happened over the last week, and I regret that I haven't journaled every day. I'm challenging myself to write updates every day, so that I can release and process my thoughts.

This is a rollercoaster ride, and I'm ready to get off. It's as if I'm stuck on it and the more I try to get the conductor's attention to tell him to stop so I can get off, the longer he keeps me on the ride and the faster he makes it go. And then, I'm not sure which part is worse, the anticipation as I'm going up the hill and wondering if I'll ever get to the top of the hill, or being consumed in the freefall of the ride.

My heart has never ached as much as it did on Monday, and I don't think it's been as broken as it is today. Knowing that things are always subject to change, Noah was having a good day on Monday, and we were going to be able to cuddle. When I arrived at the hospital, the nurse informed me his saturation levels had been dropping, and she didn't think it would be a good idea to get him out of his bed.

Every nurse responds differently when a baby has de-sating episodes—some will still let you hold them, providing the baby has become stable and remains stable for a period, and others just aren't comfortable with moving them at all. The day before, they increased some of his medicines based on his weight gain, so it was clear that holding him wasn't a good idea so he could adjust.

I had a mini-meltdown on Monday in part because of not being able to hold him. Mind you, I never put my wants and desires before Noah's best interest. My heart ached so bad just to hold him, and I couldn't. Not long after being told I couldn't hold him at all that day, an angel walked in; her name was Robin. We talked a bit, and she gave me one of the greatest gifts ever by offering and letting me hold her daughter, Emmaline. This may sound silly, but unless you've been in this situation, it probably doesn't make sense to you. However, being able to hold Emmaline helped ease the ache.

Thursday, July 30, 2009, 11:35 pm, ET

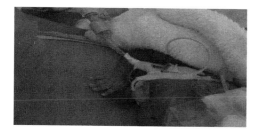

Week 6, Thursday prayer requests:
1. *Wholeness of intestines*
2. *Become and stay infection-free*
3. *Continued good growth*

Like a bumble bee

Noah had a good day overall; however, he's fighting a gastrointestinal disease called NEC (necrotizing enterocolitis). NEC is a common experience in the first few weeks of life in babies born before 32 weeks. Noah is back on antibiotics, and we've discontinued feedings since he's getting nutrients via IV. On top of the NEC, his liver isn't functioning the way it's supposed to. The way to fix the liver is by feeding, but he can't start feeding again until the NEC is cleared.

This is the first time since Noah has started feeding, that his food is being stopped. The nurses were very surprised and double checked his chart to make sure I was right in saying he's never had his feedings stopped. They said it's typical for a baby born his size to have feedings stopped several times by this age due to intolerance—what can I say? The boy likes to eat!

I was able to hold him today, which I didn't expect to happen. He is getting heavy too—if you consider three pounds heavy—I can feel the difference though!

Yesterday, when I went to sit with Noah, I knew something wasn't quite right. I was about three feet away from his incubator when an awful aroma assaulted my nose. Noah had pooped, and it wasn't his usual kind of load. The size was bigger, the consistency was different, the color was off, and the fact that I could smell it before getting to him and opening the doors to the incubator was a telltale sign for me that something was off. He had a few more poops like that. I mentioned this to the nurse, but because there wasn't any blood in his stool, she wasn't too concerned. I trust the experts—this is their world, and they've been working in it for a long time. I'm learning to trust my instincts and continuing to speak up.

I just knew something was wrong with his poop being odd, and the next day, he had blood in his stool which prompted a second x-ray today. He wasn't irritable or fussy, and he wasn't lethargic either—typical symptoms of a sick baby. He reminds me of a bumble bee—it shouldn't be able to fly because it's wings are too small for it's body weight, but no one told the bee, and that's how Noah is. Noah doesn't look or act sick, yet his body is sick. But Noah is an awesome fighter with a lot of spunk.

I'm holding onto God's Word and the promises He has given us—Knowing that all things work together for good for those who love Him and are called by His name. He's not given me a spirit of fear, but power, love, and a sound mind. My flesh and my heart may fail, but "God is the strength of my heart and my portion forever." (Ps 73:26). So I rejoice that today was a one of a kind day, and tomorrow brings a new beginning with a fresh canvas to paint.

May God continue to keep and richly bless us all.

Week 7
Branches and miracles

Sunday, August 2, 2009, 1:50 am, ET

Week 7, Sunday prayer requests:
1. *Help Indy (our old roommate) become and stay infection-free*
2. *Resume feedings ASAP*
3. *Continue good growth*
4. *Remain infection-free*

Glory be to God! Hallelujah, Hallelujah, Hallelujah— Noah is HEALED!

The NEC infection is no longer detectable in Noah's system! Both yesterday and today were wonderful days. When I checked on him on Friday, the doctor said his film (x-ray) looked good. His bowel movements were less frequent, had a greater consistency, and had very little blood in them if any. This is a miracle; I would have been miserable if I couldn't see the goodness of the Lord. Noah hasn't had any desaturation episodes; he's been self-recovering, his lungs look and sound better, and he needs less ventilator support.

Thank you for being a branch

Thank you to each of you who continue to pray with us and pray Noah gets through this. Although I don't know you personally, I thank you for being "branches"—extensions from God's tree. Seeing Noah today is like looking at a different baby. Even though he's dropped a few ounces of fluid weight, he's remarkable and feisty as can be.

The nurse mentioned last night that we'll be able to put clothes on Noah soon. This is a huge deal because it means Noah is working on keeping his body temperature up on his own. With that said, we'll be coming off the ventilator very, very soon.

I am so thankful and grateful for God's miraculous work and you saints for your relentless prayers.

Monday, August 3, 2009, 9:50 pm, ET

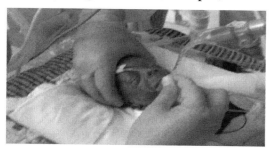

Week 7, Monday prayer requests:
1. *Read Psalm 47*
2. *Strength to move to CPAP or nasal cannula for breathing support*
3. *Remain infection-free*
4. *Resume feedings on Friday*

Another miracle—Noah is off the ventilator. He extubated (loss of ventilator tube placement) on Sunday morning.

Tuesday, August 4, 2009, 9:44 am, ET

Week 7, Tuesday prayer requests:
1. *Remain infection-free*
2. *Start feedings ASAP*
3. *Continue developing lung strength and capacity*
4. *Help Indy become and stay infection-free, and give her strength and wholeness in her body*

Noah can cry!

Yesterday was a full day for Noah. He started occupational therapy to keep his muscles from getting stiff (his arms definitely aren't stiff; he does plenty of swatting and swinging!) As he gets more stable on the SiPap machine, I'll begin doing exercises with him. He has gotten much better with tolerating people getting in his space and messing with him. He did get overstimulated yesterday and had a few desaturation episodes, but at least I know it was the overstimulation that caused them now. He's getting so big and filling out all over!

When mom and I went back to visit with Noah last night, we heard him cry. It was a wonderful sound to hear. While holding him, he was pulling up his head—he can't hold it up yet of course, but he sure can move it in the direction he wants. He actually looked like he was rooting a bit. We aren't to the point where I can try breastfeeding yet, but I'm sure he realizes I have something for him!

Noah is also setting his standard with how he likes to be put to sleep. When he's on his tummy, he wants his bottom to be patted, and while he's on his back or sides, he likes us to stand up and hold the paci (pacifier) in his mouth. Noah already has his grandmother wrapped around his itty bitty fingers—she always wants to give him sugar water—it's a real treat for babies, especially when they have to do painful procedures such as eye exams or IVs. It's the equivalent of my chocolate fix.

Please continue to pray for us, Indy, and her family. Right now she's in a curve in the road and needs all the prayers and support we can give. Her parents and grandparents are so precious and sweet—we truly support each other. I gave her a card that said, "When life gives you lemons… throw them back." We can't throw lemons, but we need a moment to release some frustration. I think we'll set up a day to throw water balloons.

I went to my first Mary Kay meeting in two months last night; it felt really good. I wasn't sure how I was going to handle being around a lot of people and having to answer a lot of questions, but it felt good and right to be back. The Mary Kay unit is like an extended family, and the love that's there feels wonderfully comforting—I'm thankful and so grateful for them.

Friday, August 7, 2009, 7:24 am, ET

Week 7, Friday prayer requests:
1. *Read Psalm 51*
2. *Remain infection-free*
3. *Healing to his liver and all vital organs*
4. *Resume feedings*
5. *Help Indy become and stay infection-free*
6. *Help Phil come off his ventilator*

A breath of fresh oxygen

Noah is on nasal cannula support now. He's breathing on his own and is supported by oxygen alone. Thank you, Jesus! He's not able to eat yet because his intestines aren't completely healed, but he's getting nutrition. He's been swollen the past couple of days, but it's starting to taper off as well due to a diuretic. He's also staying up for longer intervals, day and night. He was up and looking around for half of our three-hour visit yesterday.

WOW! How great is my God?! Our God?! God has certainly moved into Noah's room this week. He has hit three major milestones and is progressing well. He self-extubated Sunday morning, meaning he deliberately pulled out the endotracheal tube—the miracle is that he had to get the tube re-taped and that happened around 1:00 am on Sunday (mom and I were there watching them do it). Noah wasn't happy about the re-taping at all and was fighting it so much that three of them had to hold his arms and legs down with a sheet.

When I talked to the nurse at 8:30 am, she told me he had pulled it out—GLORY be to God! He really was tired of the tube, and it was time to come out, so he went from the ventilator to the SiPap. The SiPap machine gives his lung pressure support and a backup breathing rate (so it breathes so many times a minute for him, above what he does on his own). On Wednesday, Noah progressed to the CPAP machine, which doesn't give him any breaths, but it gives his lungs pressure support when inhaling and exhaling.

Seeing Noah's whole, handsome face

Yesterday, I got to see his *whole* face because he went to the nasal cannulas—it looks just like when people walk around with an O2 tank. I was so excited to be able to see my baby's whole face, and actually see what he looks like! And as I expected, he is extremely handsome. He's so sweet and so much more comfortable without all the breathing machines. I know the machines are there to help, but babies have a way of knowing when enough is enough. Noah rests so much better now, doesn't fight nearly as much, and he doesn't look stressed. He used to look stressed, even while he was sleeping, but not anymore!

Now that he's off the machines it's much easier to get him in and out of bed without tangling up the wires. We've been holding each other every day this week. Yesterday was just precious; we looked and talked to each other for 20 minutes. Noah will lift his head and place it where he wants it (usually lower on my chest); I think he's trying to get to the milk supply!

One of the nurses, made him two blankets with his name embroidered on them—they love him in the nursery!

We've come a long way baby!

Friday, August 7, 2009, 10:53 pm, ET

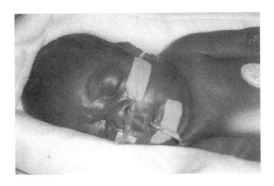

This afternoon, Noah got started on Pedialyte, an electrolyte drink for children. This is great news because it means his intestines are doing much better. He's still having some apneic episodes when he forgets to breathe, but he had those on the other machines as well. It's more critical for him now though since he's breathing on his own.

Noah had a good day today. He has a big test to pass this weekend—feed, breathe, and stay infection-free. He has already surpassed a multitude of hurdles already, so I'm confident and know that he'll pass this one as well.

We got to hold each other today and that time just gets sweeter and sweeter each day—our favorite thing to do together is take naps. Noah often smiles very hard and laughs when we're together. He also uses this time to strengthen his neck muscles; he constantly picks his head up and puts it where he'd like it to go.

The nurses have been a God send this week; I'm so glad he was taken care of by nurses who've had him before and were willing to give him a chance on the SiPap, CPAP, and the nasal cannula—look at us now! Our nurses have been absolute angels, and I appreciate them so much. They take care of Noah as if he were their own birth child (*"he does have favor,"* Luke 2:52 and Prov 3:4). Another nurse, made him a name card with the meaning of his name and a scripture. I love the name card so much I asked her to make a second name card with Samuel, his middle name on it. It is such a wonderful ministry gift she has—it's simple, but it means so much to me.

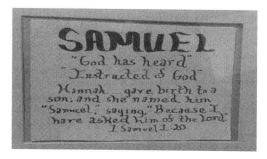

Oh, and an update on Indy, she's off the ventilator now!

I'm looking forward to the great things tomorrow holds... until then.

And God Remembered Noah

Week 8
Forward and sideways

Tuesday, August 11, 2009, 12:04 pm, ET

Week 8, Tuesday prayer requests:
1. *Read Psalm 56*
2. *Remain infection-free*
3. *Tolerate feedings*
4. *Reduce swelling in lower body*
5. *Continued good growth and development*
6. *Indy and Phil*
7. *Strength and wisdom for my decision-making*

Everything is on the up

Praise God, we're on the upswing of things. Noah started on breast milk again yesterday and he's getting 2.3 ml. every four hours. His lung and intestine x-rays are looking good, and his liver function is doing much better. The doctors were surprised by how great his liver function tests came out. To this, I say, thank you, Jesus! The apneic episodes aren't as frequent as before, so his brain is working things out.

Indy is off of the ventilator and is on CPAP now, so she'll be going to the nasal cannula before long. I got to see her with her eyes open the other night; she is beyond cute and precious. I like to call her Princess Indy.

Baby Phil is doing excellent—he's off the ventilator and on the nasal cannula, and I can see his whole face and how cute he is too. He looks like his grandmother and a little bit like his mom.

I am so proud of Noah and all of the things he's doing. He is a remarkable baby and just so smart. I've finally felt a weight lift off of my chest when it comes to Noah's prognosis. I know in my heart of hearts that he is and is going to be just fine, yet I'm starting to get flooded with overwhelming thoughts for when he comes home; *How am I going to take care of him? What will he need?* I'm constantly reciting Romans 12:2, and avoiding becoming conformed, but transformed by the renewing of my mind; knowing that God shall supply all of our needs. Knowing everything will work out and not even entertaining the "what ifs."

Through this experience, my faith and trust in God have gone to another level. I know I'm nothing and can do nothing without Him. Seeing and believing that I can do all things through Christ who strengthens me. I'm expecting great things this week—for Noah to start nipple feeding, an increase in customers and Mary Kay business opportunities, and a successful parent support group meeting.

Thank you, Lord, for your faithfulness; I'm forever grateful.

This picture is of Princess Indy and her Mom, Jenny.

Thursday, August 13, 2009, 9:51 am, ET

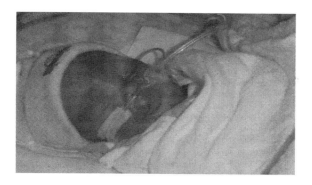

I took this photo yesterday; it's my favorite one yet. Even though Noah can fuss and cut up, he's such a sweet and pleasant little boy.

Week 8, Thursday prayer requests:
1. Read Psalm 58
2. Remain infection-free
3. Brain regulation
4. Continued good growth

We get to wear clothes!

Noah is 8 weeks old, and he hit the 4 pound mark! We actually hit it a few days ago, but I've been a little slow on writing my updates. Noah weighs 4.2 pounds now, some of which is from fluid retention, so it's not a true weight. I haven't been sharing his weight because I know he still has some fluid ounces to lose, but he's well on his way to a true 4 pounds.

Noah is in clothes! You might wonder why I'm so excited about Noah being able to wear clothes. It's an incredible milestone. A few weeks after being in the hospital one of the nurses told me not to be alarmed, but to be happy if I walk in one day and see Noah wearing clothes because that means they're working on him maintaining his own body temperature.

Once babies are able to hold their own temperature, they can move from the incubator to the bassinet, which is one step closer to coming home. Today, I walked into the nursery and over to his bed and saw that he had on a hat, a t-shirt, and was wrapped in a couple of blankets and I just began to laugh. Then I caught myself—I asked the nurse if I should be excited or if he was dressed because he was cold. She reassured me that clothes were a good thing and they're letting him work on maintaining his own body temperature. When babies are in the incubator, there's a warmer that works to keep the baby's temperature in normal range.

Even with achieving milestones, our days are still trying. I believe Noah is out of the most critical stage, but we still have some major issues to overcome and outgrow.

While we were holding each other yesterday, Noah had a major episode—his heart rate and oxygen saturation dropped dramatically. Stimulation normally helps him remember to breathe and then he comes back. Yesterday though, it was taking longer than usual for him to come back, and he went pale on me. It's normal for preemies to have seizures because of their immature central nervous system. This is why I listed brain regulation as a prayer request. The brain is command central; without it, we don't function.

Noah has had and still is having a lot of things introduced to him. He has to figure out how to handle it simultaneously. My heart goes out to parents with older children who have epilepsy.

There are no words to describe how you feel watching your child have a seizure.

The doctors aren't calling these "episodes" seizures, but that's what they seem like to me. Yet, to God be the glory, because He works everything out.

Saturday, August 15, 2009, 11:44 am, ET

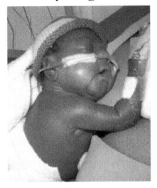

Week 8, Saturday prayer requests:
1. *Read Psalm 61*
2. *Remain infection-free*
3. *Lung development*
4. *Brain development*

Hurry up and wait

Noah's feedings were doubled yesterday, and he's handling them well. He went back on SiPap last night; he was having too many episodes and draining himself trying to keep up, so they decided to give him a rest by going back on SiPap (the machine that gives him pressure to his lungs and back up breaths). He's not in clothes right now either because his body temperature wasn't staying up.

This isn't a backward step; it's a side step. Noah did an excellent job this week. He's been off the ventilator for two weeks now, on the nasal cannula for a week, he started eating again, tolerating the feeds, making bowel movements without assistance, and he had clothes on for two days! I'm very proud of him and understand that he needed a rest—he's not supposed to be here yet, he's supposed to be inside of me still.

Yesterday was hard. I know God says He won't give us more than we can bear, yet I felt like I'd reached my breaking point. Noah had episode after episode, and it was taking longer and longer to bring him back.

We're in the "hurry up and wait" phase right now. I had a good conversation with the older Dr. B; he doesn't think the episodes are seizures, yet more from immature lungs and lung disease. He said Noah's blood gases look good, his bowels look and sound good, his head seems fine (no changes), he's tolerating feedings, and there's no sign of infection. He mentioned we might have to go back to CPAP or SiPap to help with pressure, but only time will tell. I was fine while having this conversation with the doctor, I didn't cry, and I held my composure because I know that Noah was just asking for a little help. The doctor also thinks we should start Noah's exercises again, as long as he'll tolerate them.

The nurse, asked me if I wanted to hold Noah, and I hesitated. I never hesitate to hold him; I'm always eager to hold my baby boy. I was afraid that I was causing the episodes from the stimulation. The doctor thinks Noah does better when he's stimulated (less apneic) so, I held him.
He's becoming such a chunkster and so adorable! Since he wasn't in clothes, we kangaroo cuddled—skin to skin feels so good with him. While I was holding him, he

started having an episode and went into a tailspin. As soon as his levels came up and the stimulation stopped, he went right back down and into another episode and they had to bag him (bagging opens the lungs and gets the oxygen further into the lungs). I was so done after that. It wasn't so much seeing them bag him, it's the adrenaline and the stress that goes along with it, being there with him, through the episodes and watching them get worse over the last three days is what did it.

The nurse thinks the repeat episodes are coming from Noah not having enough CO_2; she believes he's blowing it all off. Carbon dioxide levels tell the brain when we need to breathe. Basically, Noah isn't having a good exchange of O_2 and CO_2.

Don't get weary in well-doing

I normally pump breastmilk after holding Noah and make sure he gets fresh milk every day. But that didn't happen yesterday; I let him have frozen milk. I just felt I had to get out of the hospital or I was going to lose it all together. As I was leaving I ran into another nurse—she was a God send, so funny and so sweet. Today, she gave me the encouragement I needed. She reminded me of the importance of pumping and how good it is for Noah, and that this is just a phase we'll both get through.

I was at the point where I was going to stop pumping; I was feeling greatly discouraged. Many women prefer to formula feed for many reasons that I don't agree with, but that's their choice. I so want to breastfeed, and it just seems so far away, and I wonder if we'll ever get there. I'm doing everything I can to keep my milk supply up (except resting—I try, but it's challenging). People add their thoughts and opinions on breastfeeding and share from their breastfeeding experience, and most aren't encouraging. I know people don't mean any harm and aren't trying to be insensitive, but they had a choice and a chance to try; I haven't had that chance yet. I've chosen to pump, hoping we'll have the chance to breastfeed. The scripture that continues to come to mind is, "Don't get weary in well doing." I hold on to this reminder and expect that the day is not far off that I'll be able to put Noah to my breast.

I journal to capture these precious days of Noah's life, reflect on where we've been, release what I'm feeling— the good, the bad, and the ugly, and have a record of the prayers God has answered. I know, trust, and believe that Noah is whole, will come home soon, and will lead a healthy productive life; it's the process that's challenging.

Saturday, August 15, 2009, 9:59, pm, ET

I've never been happier to be leaking!

Last night's visit was very refreshing for both of us. It was my first time giving Noah a bath, and I covered him in petroleum jelly to moisturize his dry skin.

Noah's night nurse called to let me know they had put Noah back on SiPap. I'm thankful and grateful for the heads up; it makes it easier for me to deal with major changes like this ahead of time instead of getting hit with it when I walk in the door. It gives me a chance to process the information ahead of time.

I changed his diaper, and he had a nice surprise in it for me. He enjoyed his bath; he kept all his levels and numbers up and didn't fuss. I believe I enjoyed bath time more than he did. Just as I was finishing drying Noah off, I began to leak from my left breast! I was so thankful and took it as a sign to keep pumping; don't stop yet. I say this because it has been tedious to get milk from the left side. I'm lucky if I get 2 ounces from the left side; it's usually half, or less than half that of the right side every time. So, for me to leak is unusual in itself, but to leak from the left side, that was God.

I got to hold Noah again last night while his nurse changed his bed. Once the bed was changed, I went to pump as much milk as I could from the left side. I left my pump and all materials downstairs in the car, so I was hand pumping. It's pretty funny to think about and probably funnier to have seen the process—I was literally milking myself. And I must say, I was truly proud of myself for pumping over an ounce of milk from the left side by hand. It's okay to laugh at me because I was surely laughing at myself! I'm sure I'll have more bloopers to share as time goes on.

The evening was much better than the day. I left refreshed, renewed, and committed to pumping. Noah rested peacefully and had an episode-free night.

And God Remembered Noah

Week 9
Tuning into the "preemie channel"

Tuesday, August 18, 2009, 1:21 am, ET

Week 9, Tuesday prayer requests:
1. *Read Psalm 62*
2. *Remain infection-free*
3. *Brain regulation*
4. *Lung development*

A full kind of birthday

Noah has had a full and busy day. He had an EEG
test (a test that detects electrical activity in your brain)
and exercised with occupational therapy first thing this
morning.

He met with the orthopedic doctor, about his left leg
and will have a follow-up sometime later. He had asth-
ma medicine and respiratory treatments too. His lower
body is still swollen, but the swelling in his legs is finally

starting to go down.

Another day down and a day closer to when we go home. When will that day be? I have no idea. Noah is two months old today, but only 35 weeks corrected (gestational) age; so he's still not supposed to be here yet—he has come a long, long way though. To celebrate Noah's two month birthday, I made cupcakes for the nursing staff—They were quite tasty if I do say so myself.

Noah is a trickster

Noah still has episodes, but they're nothing like they were last week—he'll self-correct before the nurse gets to him. He went as low as he could go tonight and that was the first time I've ever witnessed or heard that he's done that.

His grandmother said she's seen him pull this particular "trick" a couple of times; I can say tonight's episode has scared me the most thus far. I trust and have complete confidence in the nursing staff; however, that still doesn't alleviate the fact that my kid has bottomed out. Then, when Noah comes back around, he's stretching and looking around as if to say, "What's all the commotion about? What's going on? I was just dreaming, nothing serious."

We should get the results of the EEG later this week. I'll be glad and feel more at ease knowing what's potentially causing the episodes—whether it's his head, lungs, or immaturity.

Tuesday, August 18, 2009, 11:32 am, ET

God helped me get on the "preemie channel"

The rest of Noah's day and night went well. He went to sleep after I left, and his nurse said he was quiet for the rest of the night. He didn't have an episode until this morning, around 8:30 am when the respiratory therapist came in to give him his treatment.
He weighs a whopping 4.5 pounds now! The diuretic is finally working and taking some fluid off.

I finally got it. Dr. S, the neonatologist, told me about six weeks ago to shift my mind from the newborn channel to the preemie channel. The preemie channel means that Noah's progress will be slow, the process isn't going to be a quick fix, and he isn't going home anytime soon. So, after two months, the doctor's advice has finally sunk in that we very well may be in the hospital past my due date, September 20.

Last night was my wake up call. It's not that Noah isn't doing well, because he is. However, he has so many other milestones to conquer before we can think about coming home, and that's okay. I want him to come home as healthy as he can be and not a day before he's ready. There are three major things Noah has to do before coming home:

1. Breathe on his own
2. Eat
3. Hold his body temperature

So far, we've tried 2 of the 3, and we're just not there yet. It's not a matter of what the doctors and nurses can do; it's up to Noah and God to work these things out. I believe God has brought him this far and I know He will continue to see Noah and me through.

"I will bless the Lord at all times, and His praise shall continually be in my mouth. My soul shall make her boast in the Lord, the humble shall hear thereof. O magnify the Lord with me! I sought the Lord, and he heard me, and delivered me from all my fears." (Psalm 34:1-4)

Wednesday, August 19, 2009, 12:05 am, ET

Week 9, Wednesday prayer requests:

1. *Read Psalm 63*
2. *Remain infection-free*
3. *Brain regulation*
4. *Accelerated development*

The chunkster has a double chin!

Noah weighs 4.5 pounds, and has a double chin! How funny is that? The swelling is going down in his legs and around his face. He's on a second seizure medicine now. The EEG didn't record any seizure activity, but Noah didn't have an episode while they were doing the test. He did have an episode with me while I was holding him, and even the nurse mentioned that it looked like a seizure (he had some jerking arm motion as he his numbers were coming back up). The EEG did say Noah's gestational development was at 32 weeks. When the test was done, he was at the beginning of 35 weeks gestational age, so there's some underdevelopment, but he can catch up. Noah will be getting his two-month vaccinations soon; I just signed the paperwork for those tonight.

"Hear my cry, O God; listen to my prayer. From the end of the earth will I cry out to You, when my heart is over-whelmed and fainting; lead me to the rock that is higher than I." (Psalm 61: 1-2)

Rose-colored glasses can be a helpful tool

I didn't like the doctor's report for the cause of the episodes; therefore, I won't repeat it. I'm not in denial, and I don't look through rose colored glasses all the time, yet I'm careful of what I speak sometimes. I do believe there's life and death in the power of the tongue and once words are released, you can't take them back.

The episodes and difficulty Noah was experiencing was most likely due to the brain damage sustained from the severe brain bleed. It was likely his body was shutting down due to the trauma sustained pre, during, and post delivery. It seemed too much for his body to bounce back from.

Words are very powerful

Through this passage of life, God has placed many angels in our path. One asked to be Noah's primary nurse. This means that whenever she's working, she'll take care of Noah (and two other babies, but she'll always care for him). Being a primary nurse is such an awesome endeavor because she'll be with the same kids every shift, she'll become even more attached, and she'll need to deal with me and my meltdowns.

The great thing about having primary nurses is the continuity of care Noah will receive. Can you imagine having a different nurse care for you every day and every shift? This was our story for a little while, and I tell you, enough is enough. It's hard trying to explain time and time again what Noah likes, dislikes, how he is with episodes, and so on. I know they create the nurse schedule with some continuity in mind, and it doesn't always work in our favor, but it's wonderful to have nurses volunteer to take care of your child. I love seeing how attached Noah gets to the nurses; I promise he has his favorites. He doesn't act up quite as bad with his favorites as he does with some of the others.

Noah is so loved in and out of the nursery, and it's such a blessing. Although this is not the route I would have selected for myself, I'm thankful for the opportunity to learn how to wait on God, stretch and grow personally and spiritually, and meet a host of wonderful and awesome people.

Friday, August 21, 2009. 6:05 am, ET

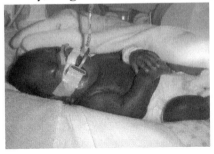

Week 9, Friday prayer requests:

- *Read Psalm 64*
- *Brain development, restoration, and regulation*
- *Remain infection-free*
- *Tolerate feedings*

My biggest fear

Noah weighs 4 pounds, 10 ounces. He's on the ventilator, antibiotics, and will start feeding again later today. On Wednesday night, Noah took a turn for the worse causing him to go back on the vent. By God's grace, Noah is stable and has been for the past 36 hours. We had our first slumber party—mommy staying at the hospital more than 24 hours. He had his third eye exam yesterday; all seems well with his eyes, and he'll have his eyes checked again in two weeks. Noah rests a lot, but he's burnt up all his energy trying to stay alive. He's responsive and awake periodically. We need a miracle from head to toe, and I know God is able.

...

A decision no parent should ever have to make

I just lost an hour's worth of journaling, so I have to recompose myself and retype.

The past two days have been the most trying days I've ever encountered in my life. I had to make a decision that no person or parent should have to make. When I left Noah on Wednesday afternoon, he was doing fine. He had a major episode at shift change that morning and had two more episodes before I got to the hospital, but those didn't require as much stimulation to get him back. We had a very good visit. We cuddled for a long time and had no episodes. The older Dr. B was on service today, and we had a no-fluff and real conversation. I was concerned about the type and frequency of these episodes, the lack of engagement, and reduced activity Noah was experiencing. I asked about what were we looking at and our worst case scenario. His words weren't what I was expecting to hear. Worst case scenario, we put Noah back on the ventilator. I was good with that as I thought I'd have to decide whether to stop further interventions and let Noah go.

One of the sweetest ladies and nurses I've ever met, told me she'd take good care of Noah, and told me to get some rest. I went home to take a nap, because I've just been drained. The phone was ringing and jolted me from my sleep. I couldn't answer it in time. It was the hospital and they left a message—I need to think about signing a DNR.

The doctor told me Noah had taken a turn for the worse and they'd need to put him back on the ventilator. He told me I had two options and asked about a DNR (do not resuscitate) because of the amount of work it was taking to get Noah back, and the fact that he had coded and needed to be bagged the past three episodes. Each episode was worse than the last and requiring longer and more vigorous stimulation to bring him back. I told the doctor I couldn't make that decision at the moment and asked what my other option was. He told me they could put him on the ventilator, so I said, "Do that, I'm on my way down there."

My worst fear had come true; my baby is checking out. As we were staring death in the face, my cry was, "Please God keep him!"

When I got to the hospital, the staff had Noah as stable as he could be. I had to wait in the family waiting room for what seemed like eternity but was more like 20 minutes before I could see him. While waiting, Jenny had come to see Indy, and I told her what was going on. I was at a loss. We were in this situation before, but our places were flip-flopped. She prayed for Noah, and for me—I was at the end of my rope and struggling in my faith that Noah would pull through.

As I walked into his room and looked into the eyes of the doctor, the unit clerk, the nurses, and therapists all I saw was sadness, despair, and concern. I'm a detail person, so I asked, "What happened?" His nurse told me as they were changing shifts, his numbers dropped, and they had to bag him. She bagged him for 30 minutes thinking it would get him through that time, but he just bottomed out and started shutting down. They had to bag, do chest compressions, and give a shot of epinephrine to bring Noah back.

In hindsight, he coded—you know, a "code blue." The nurse described the disarray and disheveled state Noah's incubator was in, due to the immediate and intense intervention required when I arrived, and she just couldn't let me see things like that.

The bigger the storm, the bigger the rainbow

As I visited with Noah, we talked; just him, me, and God. I told Noah how proud I am of him and what a smart and handsome boy he is. I said, "Noah, I love you very much, so very much and it's okay. I'm not giving up on you. You let mommy know what you want to do. If you're tired and you want to go be with Jesus, it's okay. I don't want you to go, but it's okay. Whether you stay here with me or you stay with Jesus, it's going to be alright." As I talked to him, he opened and closed his eyes a few times. As he looked at me, Noah had more life in his eyes then than he did the past couple of days.

We had the chance to cuddle and what a wonderful time we had. It was funny to me that the nurse and respiratory therapist that were with me the very first time I held Noah were the same ones there on our potential last hold. I'm thankful they were there and I reminded them of our first hold. They're so compassionate and love the babies in that unit. They take such great care of Noah and me; they would pray for and over him when they had him. What more can a mother ask for than someone to take care of your child as if they were their own?

That cuddle time felt just as good if not better than the first time. All I could do was give praise to God for keeping Noah and pray over him while I held him. At that moment, I experienced a new level of trust.

I trust You, Lord with my whole heart. This is not the path that I would have chosen, but You are all knowing. You know my heart and my desire for Noah, but no matter the outcome I will trust You.

I rested in the chair next to Noah's incubator until the next shift change, came home, showered, changed my clothes, and went back to the hospital. He didn't have any other episodes that night, and that was my sign to toss out the DNR papers. We were going to fight together—we're in it for the long haul.

His nurse on Thursday told me she was praying for us her whole way to work not knowing if she'd be taking care of him when she arrived. She was so encouraging! She said, "Naomi, rainbows can't exist without a storm and the bigger the storm, the bigger the rainbow." What a true statement. She also shared a list of scriptures that she often reads. We are blessed to have such God-fearing staff in that unit, and those who aren't afraid to share their faith.

"I am the Lord, the God of all mankind. Is anything too hard for me?" (Jeremiah 32:27)

Saturday, August 22, 2009, 10:37 am, ET

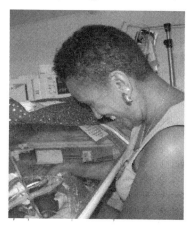

Week 9, Saturday prayer requests:
1. *Read Psalm 65*
2. *Accelerated development*
3. *Brain regulation*
4. *Remain infection-free*
5. *Transition from ventilator to SiPap*
6. *My milk production*

Building our reserves

Noah is stable and weaning off the ventilator. He started feeding again yesterday afternoon and is tolerating that well. He was started back on antibiotics, and he's had no episodes since Wednesday at 7:00 pm—thank you, Jesus. He's swollen from all the bagging, but it's starting to go down.

Yesterday, Friday, was a good day. Noah has been stable

the last two and a half days. He had an eye exam on Thursday and tolerated that very well, better than anyone expected. His eyes are fine and will be checked again in two weeks. We had our primary care nurse yesterday, and I was very happy she was back—she encourages me so much! She doesn't have to say anything, yet I know she cares for us so much and is praying for us all the time. She listens with a servant's heart. She got us another paci (I really wish I knew who took his other ones). She cuts them to fit even with the ventilator.

Noah looks better and is resting better. He's working with the vent, breathing 3-50 breaths over the machine which is good—very good. His blood gas levels have been good, enough to decrease the support. He has tolerated people going in and out of his bed, changing his diaper, getting blood drawn, respiratory treatments, baths, and everything else.

It looks like he's built up a reserve of energy. He's like a completely different baby, and with God's help, he'll continue improving. Noah has such a will and drive to live. He continues to amaze the doctors. They may not be optimistic, but I am.

Grandmother changed Noah's diaper on Thursday. She'll have to fill me in on the details, but the parts I saw were hilarious—I think she needs a little more practice. She put the diaper on backward and wanted to leave it like that! Granted, the diapers are so small, and you have to stick your hands through two holes in the incubator, it's incredibly awkward. At least she didn't get peed on in the confusion.

We are keeping on, and I'm encouraged.

"So do not fear, for I am with you; do not be dismayed, for I am your God. I will strengthen you and help you; I will uphold you with my righteous right hand." (Isaiah 41:10)

Week 10
Come to Jesus meetings &
wishes of coming home

Sunday, August 23, 2009, 1:56 am, ET

Week 10, Sunday prayer requests:

1. *Read Psalm 66*
2. *Excellent transition from vent to SiPap*
3. *Remain infection-free*
4. *Accelerated development*

Noah continues his trickster ways

Noah had a very good day today. He's been resting well, but responsive when he needs to be. He's back to his old tricks—pulling on the ventilator tube; so he's ready to get that thing out of him. He has done an excellent job with self-recovery, meaning he hasn't needed nurse or staff intervention to come out of an episode. Sunday is the big day! We go back to SiPap, and I believe Noah will tolerate it like a champ!

Noah looks like a different baby, or maybe I should say he's acting like a different baby. He had his own "come to Jesus" meeting, and has done a complete turnaround. He's controlling his breathing so much better and he is also not as puffy. I have high expectations for tomorrow.

Tuesday, August 25, 2009, 12:35 am, ET

Week 10, Tuesday prayer requests:

1. *Read Psalm 69*
2. *Remain infection-free*
3. *Accelerated development*
4. *Hold body temperature*
5. *Tolerate feedings*
6. *Mommy's milk production*

Noah is doing excellent!

Thank you, Jesus! He had his feedings increased today, so he's eating about 6 ounces a day, starting today. They stopped antibiotics and fluids today as well, and they took the PICC line out. His heart rate hasn't dropped, and he hasn't needed much help with maintaining his O2 levels. He wore clothes today and is working to hold his body temperature. Today is a very good day.

On Sunday, Noah was taken off of the ventilator and went to SiPap; he has done very well with the transition. He's still weaning from this machine; so maybe, just maybe he'll be on the nasal cannula by the end of the week.

Indy is doing well; she weighs 2 pounds, 12 ounces. She's on the nasal cannula and doing well. She is so cute and very alert. Her parents are doing good too. Please continue to lift them up in your prayers (and baby Phil) when you pray for Noah.

The past couple of days have been good ones. On Sunday, I was a bit anxious because we were coming off the ventilator. I think the reality of this hit me right before I ministered through a mime at church.

Noah, I love you and I'm proud of you

There was uncertainty about how Noah would tolerate and handle being taken off of the ventilator. Before Noah was transitioned off of the vent I talked to the doctor and again had to decide whether to approve a DNR—my answer was no, and he should go back on the vent if he didn't tolerate the SiPap. I asked the nurse to tell Noah that I love him, that I'm proud of him, and that Jesus will help him. It was so hard to say these words. However, I'm thankful that I felt comfortable and confident that she'd tell him. I feel so blessed to have the staff that we have because there are many, many units that don't have a Jesus-loving staff. It's such a testimony that once Noah was on SiPap; he didn't want the settings that they put him on—he wanted less O2 support!

Thank you, Auntie Judy, for the prayer you left us. I believe Wednesday was the last episode. I think this was Noah's "come to Jesus meeting" and he met God in a new way that night. I'm just thankful and rejoicing that all is well.

We had a new nurse today; I was a bit hesitant about having a new nurse. You know, I figure we've been here for nine weeks and some days, we shouldn't get a new nurse, and I should have met all the nurses by now. I wasn't thrilled about the new nurse situation, but God knows what we need—she is sweet, easy-going, family-friendly, and very knowledgeable.

Noah was in clothes when I went in today—hooray! They're working to see if he's ready to hold his temperature without the incubator helping him (he has to be able to hold his temperature on his own before he can come home). He was all bundled up, and you could barely see his face, but he's still so cute and sweet.

I have no idea when we get to go home, but I trust and believe each day we get a step closer. Noah weighs 4 pounds, 14 ounces now, though his true weight is probably 4 pounds, 10 ounces since he's still holding fluid. I'm betting we'll hit 5 pounds, this week—he's such a big boy!

Tuesday, August 25, 2009, 10:17 am, ET

Noah had a great night last night

He tolerated his feedings; he gets 11 ml. an hour. He's on continuous feeding into his intestines, so he gets 44 ml. every 4 hours. He has to figure out breathing on his own before the feedings can go back to his stomach. They don't want to risk him refluxing while on breathing support—this is a bad combination.

Noah got really hot last night, so they lifted the top of the incubator. He maintained his body temperature with no or little assistance! Thank you, Lord, for the work you continue to do. Since Noah is doing well in the body temperature department, he'll be moving to a big boy bed! He may still need some help holding his temperature, and there are heat packs they can put on him, but we're in the phase of training his brain to do it by itself, and he's off to a good start.

I'm so proud of Noah. Our room is at capacity—nine babies, including a set of twins, and we have some whoppers in there—some babies are 7-9 pounds! With so many babies it's rare to have a quiet moment, but through all the noise Noah is figuring things out.

His new big boy bed might pose a decorating issue for me. Right now Noah is surrounded by traced cutouts of feet. I traced the feet of some of the younger kids at church and put Bible verses on them and have them inside his bed. The new bed looks like a jail cell. Oh well, this gives me another opportunity to be creative. I'm just thankful we're moving up and closer to coming home.

Noah lost a little weight; he's 4 pounds, 10 ounces—this is a wonderful thing! He's losing the fluid that he's been retaining for weeks. His bottom is not as swollen as it had been and it's not as hard. Thank you, Jesus!

"Remember, the church suffers violence, but the violent take it by force. Have you been violent today?" (Matthew 11:12)

Wednesday, August 26, 2009, 11:04 am, ET

Week 10, Wednesday morning prayer requests:

1. *Read Psalm 70*
2. *Infection-free days*
3. *Brain cell restoration*
4. *Tolerate feedings*
5. *Indy - maintain O2 levels*
6. *Nyla - no heart murmur*
7. *Phil - good growth*

First in line for a big boy bed

Noah had a good day yesterday. He's first in line on the waiting list for a big boy bed—a crib! Once he gets in the crib that means one of the other two babies will be in a bassinet. The exciting thing is that baby Phil is one of the two in a crib. How wonderful it will be for him to go to the bassinet. I got to peek at him yesterday, and he's such a big, adorable boy.

Noah did okay with holding his body temperature. He felt cold to me while I was holding him, so I put him back earlier than I did on Monday. They like for babies temperatures to stay around 37 Celsius and he was hanging out between 36.1 to 36.4 Celsius. Until he get's his body temperature up a little, he's still bundled up with a t-shirt, a gown, two blankets, and a warmer positioned above him.

He tolerated his feedings well, and they started mixing his breastmilk. He now gets 1 part breastmilk and 1 part preemie formula; this is to increase his calorie count. He'll definitely put on some more weight now that he's having a mix of formula and breastmilk. And we just got rid of the double chin from the fluid loss.

Indy is doing well. She's been having apneic episodes, so please pray that those cease, and continue to lift her parents Jenny and James in your prayers.

Nyla is the new girl on the block. She's in our old room. She was born very early and is going through some of the same things Noah and Indy have gone through.

Right now, we need to pray that the PDA (patent ductus arteriosus) stays closed. The PDA is abnormal blood flow and what causes the heart murmur, and if it doesn't close on its own, or with medicine, she'll have to have surgery. Please pray for her mom as well. On top of having her baby this early, she lives about an hour away.

Today marks 10 weeks since the beginning of our journey. I took a little time to reread some of my entries and just cried. I'm somewhat on autopilot and don't remember a lot of things—I guess because as each day is behind me, I'm ready to move onto the next. As I read my previous entries, I thought, "Wow, we've been through all of that?!" And, *"Thank you, Lord, for where you brought us from."*

Some days are very hard and last night was no exception. It wasn't about what or where Noah was, but because it's a solo act right now. My family and friend support has been more than great, but there's still a piece missing. God knows where I am and knows what I need. I have to remind myself that He moves in His time and not mine. So, find your rest in Him, Naomi.

The joy of the Lord is my strength!

Wednesday, August 26, 2009, 10:59 pm, ET

Week 10, Wednesday night prayer requests (the same as this morning, with an addition for baby Phil):

1. *Read Psalm 70*
2. *Infection-free days*

3. *Brain cell restoration*
4. *Tolerate feedings*
5. *Indy - maintain O2 levels*
6. *Nyla - no heart murmur*
7. *Phil - He'll likely need surgery and will be moved to another local hospital*
8. *Pray for wholeness and for the surgical staff*

The crapper

Noah has had a good day. He has held his body temperature very well and even had to have a blanket peeled off of him earlier. He's tolerating his feedings and people bothering him. I can say he loves getting his CPT (chest physical therapy) and is wide-eyed during these sessions. I've named one of the respiratory therapists "the crapper" because once she's done, most babies have a poo-filled diaper. I realize it's not the most flattering name, but she does that good of a job!

My milk is coming back nicely. It's taking quite a bit of work to keep the milk factory going, but I'm hopeful and prayerful that the perseverance will pay off. I'm still holding out to be able to put Noah to breast at least once. Even when he comes home, I will more than likely have to mix my breastmilk with formula to make sure he gets enough calories.

The grandmother and I are off to do our evening visit.

Until next time.

Week 11
Welcome to my world

Tuesday, September 1, 2009, 9:16 am, ET

Week 11, Tuesday prayer requests:

1. *Read Psalm 76*
2. *Remain infection-free*
3. *Maintain body temperature*
4. *Reduce breathing assistance*
5. *Tolerate feedings*
6. *Baby Phil – for surgery go smoothly and for a speedy recovery*
7. *Indy – reduce breathing assistance*

Noah is doing great, excellent, awesome!

He has had a very good week since I last wrote. He weighs 4 pounds, 15 ounces, though I'm not sure if this is his true weight because he was on a different scale. Noah went to the pedi-crib yesterday, the jail cell looking crib, and they used a different scale to weigh him, so we'll know tomorrow if it's a true weight gain or the difference in scales.

He's up to 12 ml. an hour and his feedings are still going directly to his intestines. We might be able to start feedings back to his stomach this week. Noah had an eye exam yesterday which caused a downward spiral of a day; he had six episodes (heart rate drops and low O2 saturation) from the time he got eye drops for dilation until 12:30 am.

Noah has speech therapy coming to visit today; getting him ready to take a bottle and hopefully the breast. We've increased our exercises with occupational therapy and are working with his range of motion.

Noah and I have been keeping late nights lately so I haven't been journaling as much as I'd like. He's been doing very well and having great days. We've done some fun new things over the past several days—we had our first bath in the basin tub, and I got to wash him! I got to change his clothes too, and I'm getting better at it. We had a taste of the bottle a couple of days ago, and that was a great experience. Noah isn't quite ready to take the bottle yet, but he sucked on it a bit and is getting ready for it.

Wednesday, September 2, 2009, 11:06 pm, ET

Week 11, Wednesday prayer requests:

1. *Read Psalm 77 and 78*
2. *Remain infection-free*
3. *Tolerate feedings to stomach*
4. *Tolerate nipple (bottle) feeds*
5. *No eye surgery*

Praying for the last episode

The past two days have been good days for Noah. They increased his feedings to 12.5 ml. an hour. He's been refluxing a bit, so they're trying to get that under control. I didn't see any formula or secretions or get any spit up today, so that was good; and he had only one episode today. I'm praying that was the last one for his lifetime.

We may have to have eye surgery, and I'm hoping we don't need to. The eye doctor comes back early next week to recheck, and I believe Noah's eyes will have corrected themselves otherwise he'll have laser surgery, and that means going back on the ventilator which I don't want.

Speech therapy has been working with Noah's suck reflex and what a personality he has with that! He definitely lets them know what he likes and doesn't like and whether he's in the mood to be bothered or not. Noah will be getting his two-month shots soon; it may be before the week is out.

Dr. S talked about Noah being able to come home! I am beyond excited! Noah hit 11 weeks old today and is 37 weeks gestational age. The doctor was showing me Noah's growth chart and mentioned that he's pretty much on target and should be ready to go home around 40 weeks—that's only three weeks away!

Princess Indy is doing good; she still has episodes so pray for those to stop. She's supposed to start working with a bottle tomorrow, so be prayerful that works out too.

Baby Nyla is doing well. They don't hear the murmur anymore. She still has episodes too, so remember her and her mom in your prayers.

Baby Phil is doing excellent! He was moved to the other hospital and is supposed to have surgery, but they're holding off on that right now. He's back to the nasal cannula, which is a step up and feeding back to his stomach with no reflux. God is able and faithful.

Wow, my baby is 11 weeks old today, and I'm amazed at how big he's getting. He weighs 4 pounds, 13 ounces, and he feels every bit of it; we're knocking at the 5-pound door and will probably knock it down before the week is out.

I'm so excited the day is nearing that we may be going home. I'm trying to contain my excitement because we still have some hurdles to go over, under, around, or through and I don't want to be disappointed if we don't make it out at 40 weeks. I have to remind myself that I've trusted God this far, so don't stop now. What a blessing and testimony that we're no longer looking at way past my due date of Noah coming home, but it's very possible for him to be home by my due date.

I've got to take these next several days to finish getting his room ready and pick a pediatrician. The nurses have been preparing me for some of the issues when we get home—we can't be around a lot of people, we'll need to limit visitors, and stay home for awhile—at least until after the flu and respiratory syncytial virus (RSV) seasons pass.

I'm so thankful for God's grace and knowing that His mercy endures forever. On Monday, I shared my feelings with one of the nurses about where Noah was and how he was progressing. It was hard for a minute emotionally because there were little babies born after him but some were going home this week, and others were graduating to bassinets or coming off oxygen, and here we were having episodes again.

I understand in great detail the Bible verse, "don't grow weary with well-doing" and "the joy of the Lord is my strength." Each day offers a new beginning and a new template for God to create miracles and I've seen Him at work. God is teaching me so much through Noah and this experience. The main thing has been trusting in God, along with not comparing and understanding we each have our own pace in the race.

Understanding that when you connect the dots, they don't always go in the order you'd like, and more importantly, it's okay that they don't (thank you, LifeSkills for

Women). Everybody's picture doesn't have to look the same (and they won't); the important thing is that your picture is complete. LifeSkills is a nonprofit I used to work with. One of the lessons they taught was that when you connect the dots in a connect the dots image, you might get a picture that looks like a star, instead of the teddy bear it was supposed to look like.

I'm so excited my mom gets to hold Noah now! I almost have to jockey for position of who will hold him first. Seriously, it's a joy and honor to let her have cuddle time with Noah. They have story time, song time, and of course nap time together. My mom has been such a rock of support and comfort through this whole experience. Today's picture is of his grandmother holding him and Noah laughing and waving at her. I'd get no rest until everyone saw it, so there you go Muh.

I've also been thinking lately, how can people not believe in God? I had an in-depth lesson on what it takes to suck, swallow, and eat. Have you ever stopped to think about what's involved? Did you know there are seven steps to that process? This blows my mind.
Our bodies are wonderfully made, yet they're so complex. It's amazing that the smallest details have the biggest influence on a system's function.
Also, did you know that a baby can be so constipated they have diarrhea? Gross, I know, but I thought this was so strange and fascinating.
Welcome to my world (view) of motherhood.

Thank you, to my sisters and brothers in Christ who lift Noah and our family in your prayers. I have seen and heard the body of Christ at work and their generous, sincere, and unselfish nature. My heart is overwhelmed with the love and support shown from those who don't even know us, yet who are concerned for us and touch heaven on our behalf.

Week 12
Running a race we can't win

Monday, September 7, 2009, 12:48 am, ET

Week 12, Monday prayer requests:

1. *Read Psalm 83*
2. *Remain infection-free*
3. *No eye surgery*
4. *Tolerate stomach feedings*
5. *Tolerate the bottle*

Noah has had a remarkable week!

He got his two-month shots on Wednesday and handled them like a champ. He didn't cry until they gave him the last one, and he didn't cry long nor was it loud. I thought that might be the day he found his voice, but it wasn't. I was able to give him sweeties (sugar water) while he got the shots, so that helped to distract him. His nurse didn't want to give him the shots as much as he didn't want to get them, but they both did a good job—she is so sweet.

On Thursday, Noah went to pediflow, which is reduced oxygen support. Pediflow is actually the O2 that Noah will come home with if he needs it and not the heated high flow nasal cannula. They've been able to wean Noah down on the Pediflow, but they haven't tried to take him off of it yet; we're not quite ready for that.

Feedings started going back to his stomach on Friday, though I think my days are getting confused. They're still mixing the breastmilk and formula, and he's had a little reflux, but it's not too bad. They've already increased it from 30 to 40 ml. and on Monday they'll shorten the length of time it's delivered from an hour to 45 minutes. The reflux causes Noah to have episodes where his heart rate and oxygen saturation levels drop. After talking with the doctor, I'm at ease with the episodes. Dr. S mentioned he didn't anticipate the stomach feedings going well, but Noah has surprised him. He expected a bunch of episodes, so since he's having so few, it's not a major concern. He also said that on a scale from 1-10 they expected Noah to be a 5, but my big boy was a 9-9.5! So, Dr. S is very pleased with Noah's behavior and progress.

The doctor came to do Noah's circumcision, but since he got his shots on the same day, they're going to hold off until Tuesday. That may be delayed again if the eye doctor comes back on Tuesday as well. No need to stress him (or his mother) all the way out. I learned there are two ways to do a "circ" (as they call it), and one seems a little more humane. The one Noah will have is called a plastibell; it's a plastic cap they put on the penis and will fall off with the foreskin in a couple of days. I'll read up on it before he has this done.

Oh yes! We have hit 5 pounds, twice! Noah went from 5 pounds to 4 pounds, 14 ounces then back to 5 pounds, 1 ounce last night. He's still small but filling out so nicely. He's feeling like a bag of sugar with all that weight on him.

I also found out that Princess Indy weighs 3 pounds, 9 ounces—how exciting! She's really filling out and doing well.

Tuesday, September 8, 2009, 12:56 am, ET

Week 12, Tuesday prayer requests:
1. *Read Psalm 84*
2. *Remain infection-free*
3. *Tolerate feedings*
4. *No reflux*
5. *No eye surgery*

Today has been a rocky day

Noah has gone back on the heated high flow where he's getting more O2 support. He's been having more episodes today; we think it's from the reflux. They started him on two medications to help stop and prevent it, so we'll see if they help.

His hiney is doing much, much better tonight. His bottom had gotten really raw, so they made this little contraption to help it heal better and faster (they put O2 straight to his bottom). They cut a small hole in the bottom of a cup and put the tube of O2 through it and then open his diaper and put the cup to his hiney.

The swelling in his groin has gone down significantly. I've not seen that area look this good! Noah's liver function is getting better too; his eyes aren't as yellow tinged as before.

UGH, I just want familiar faces

We had a new nurse today. It's nothing personal to the nurse; however, we've been here almost three months, and I just don't want anybody new. Somebody getting Noah for the first time doesn't know what he's done, how he is now, what's normal for him, and how to respond to him. Yes, the nurses know what to do, but just like big people, little people have personalities, and Noah surely has his.

It's frustrating to field questions—questions that I spent the first six weeks answering. Maybe I was just a little testy today, and things that don't usually bother me bothered me. We had familiar faces for our night nurses and this is always exciting. One nurse always has a story to tell, and they're usually funny. She's Noah's night owl nurse; he'll stay up 'til the wee hours of the morning chatting with her. It's therapeutic for all of us to be with nurses who have a sense of humor. Even through the episodes, some of the nurses have a way of making me laugh about the situation afterward. The laughter helps the anxiety go away.

Wednesday, September 9, 2009, 12:03 am, ET

Week 12, Wednesday prayer requests:

1. *Read Psalm 85*
2. *Remain infection-free*
3. *No reflux*
4. *Tolerate bottle feeding*
5. *No eye surgery*

Noah has had a decent day today; the latter half was better than the beginning

Noah had a few episodes today that scared all of us in the room. These episodes aren't anywhere near as bad as the dramatic one that happened a few weeks ago though. To help prevent reflux, they've jacked Noah's bed way up to about a 45-degree angle. It looks like he's about to go somewhere, but whatever it takes to reduce the reflux, I'm game. Neither doctor came to see him today so no word on the eyes or the circumcision.

The swelling in his bottom has gone down; it was a little more swollen tonight, but it's still down. We enjoyed a nice time cuddling tonight and actually made it through reading one whole book, and Noah stayed awake. It's a cute book called, "Pajama Time." I think I liked it more than he did though.

So we pray and look forward to tomorrow being a better day.

Thursday, September 10, 2009, 12:29 am, ET

Week 12, Thursday prayer requests:

1. *Read Psalm 85*
2. *Eyes repair themselves*
3. *Remain infection-free*
4. *Tolerate feeds/no reflux*
5. *Reduce swelling in groin area and feet*
6. *Indy-continued good growth*

He's an entertainer!

WOW… It's been 12 weeks since Noah was born. He now weighs 5 pounds, 5 ounces, and what a big boy he is! He is staying up longer and is more alert these days. He's also a pretty content baby; while awake he just looks around, sucks his pacifier (if someone will stand there and hold it—like mommy), looks around some more, yawns, laughs, smiles, laughs some more, and then goes back to sleep.

He has some new facial expressions like puckering up his lips and opening his mouth like a fish. It's so funny to sit and watch him; he's quite the entertainer.

Noah is still having the apneic episodes. I'm not sure what attributed to the one I witnessed today; either reflux, eye drops, or possibly both. Some episodes are worse than others, and I'm not sure why. Noah had an eye exam this afternoon, and the doctor will be back to check in another week. Thank you, Lord! That means

Noah's eyes haven't gotten any worse and won't need surgery at this point. My prayer has been and continues to be that his eyes will correct themselves and he won't need surgery. I haven't shared my thoughts on this with anyone. His nurse tonight said she'd pray that his eyes would repair themselves—how awesome is that?

The swelling in his groin is rearing its ugly head again. Because the bed is raised so high to help reduce the reflux, fluid is beginning to collect in his lower extremities which frustrates me, and it's also probably painful for Noah. Unfortunately, there's no happy medium yet—I'm praying for this too.

We're 12 weeks into the race

It's hard to believe we've been at this for 12 weeks now. My heart, thoughts, and prayers go out to those who've been going through this since before we arrived.

Whenever I think I've had enough, I can't take any more, or that I'm at my breaking point, I remind myself that I know of at least one family that's been going through this longer than we have, and I pray for them. I am ready to start the next chapter outside of the hospital but have to remind myself that it will happen all in God's timing. This journey has let me revisit several Bible stories and make me thankful for who I am, and where I am.

I've felt myself getting short, tired, fed up, wanting to throw in the towel, or just disengage—but I can't. And God so gently reminds me of Moses and the Israelites and how they wandered for 40 years and how Moses endured the people all that time and continually sought God's guidance, then Noah and the amount of time it took him to build the ark and how absurd it was to build it because they didn't even know what rain was, then there's Hannah and how she remained barren year after year and continuously tormented, yet she was patient and sought God. My point, is for me to be at peace and let my mind rest and find comfort in Him. To work on His timetable and know that everything will work out. Twelve weeks, 14 or even 16 weeks are nothing compared to a year, 25 years, or even 40 years waiting for promises to be fulfilled.

I'm a step closer to picking a pediatrician; I think I have it narrowed down to two. I'm not sure what my deciding factor will be, but I'm happy with either choice (I think). I'm getting better and more comfortable with moving Noah around with all the wires. I gave him a bath tonight, and that went very well; he didn't bottom out on me (he did that before the bath). I got him bathed, dressed, and back in the bed with very little help. We had story time, paci time, and then night-night time.

I love the time we're able to spend together and all the neat things I'm learning about Noah, myself, and experiencing joy through the journey.

Thursday, September 10, 2009, 10:08 pm, ET

"Hear my cry O Lord, attend unto my prayer! From the ends of the earth will I cry out to you. When my heart is overwhelmed, lead me to the rock that is higher than I." (Psalm 61)

When will it get easier?

I thought by this point in the journey that things would be getting easier; knowing we'd still have our hurdles to clear, but closer to the end of our hospital stay. The first half of today was awful, just awful. It was to the point where I left in the middle of Noah having an episode. I just couldn't take it anymore. I couldn't stand there or sit there and watch them crank up the oxygen, stimulate him, and bag him one more time. Today I reached my breaking point.

Noah, I am so sorry

Before that point, I was, and I continue to speak life over Noah. I speak the Word to him and over him. Telling him, he's here for a purpose, and God has predestined him. No weapon formed against him shall prosper. God had known him before he formed in my womb. God knows the plans for you. And I rebuke Satan—you can't have Noah, you can't. He will live and not die. He will be whole and live a productive life.

The doctors and nurses are doing everything they can think of, and Noah is making them think (that's my boy; we don't make things easy) about how to eradicate these apneic episodes. So, Noah is back to continuous intestinal feedings, and maintenance doses of caffeine. They use caffeine as a stimulant for infants with premature lungs. It helps them "remember" to breathe, and reduces the dramatic O2 drops (episodes). They're also checking for infection.

I often check myself when I start losing it—Naomi, imagine how Noah feels. You're watching it, but he's experiencing it. How does he feel? During and after the episodes I remind myself of scriptures and the promises of the Lord and what God has done not just in Bible times, but currently. Even with all of that, I find myself at the end of me. I'm weary and mentally tired.

Running a never ending race

I need God to move; not for me, but for Noah—for Noah and me. I feel like the rug is being pulled out from under me. I feel like I'm the boy who was running a race and wanted to make his dad so proud of him. He started out strong, but then tripped and fell. He got up, brushed off his knees, ran a few more yards, and fell again. With each fall he fell further behind in the race, but each time he's gotten up, brushed himself off, and kept racing toward the finish line. Until the last time he fell, and now he's in last place.

Everyone has already crossed the finish line and they're wondering why he's getting up now; the race is over, he failed his dad. But little did anyone know his dad was on the way to pick him up and help him finish the race. I'm at THAT point. Lord, I need you to pick me up and help me finish this race with Noah. Noah inspires me— he's still running. He may need some help, he's asking for it when he needs it, but he keeps running.

My mind had been in Proverbs for most of the morning. He just planted, "His mercy endures forever." When things don't turn out the way I think they ought, His mercy endures forever. When there's no explanation, rhyme or reason of today's events, His mercy endures forever. When the doctors have done all they can do, His mercy endures forever. When we anticipate the worst, His mercy endures forever.

These thoughts were a breakthrough for me. I found the encouragement I need. Thank you, Lord, for your Word!

I'm so thankful for the Caring Bridge website, and I'm oh so grateful to those who leave us messages.

Kelly P., I've not had the pleasure of meeting you yet, but I thank you for your note today. You spoke my thoughts of earlier today. The reference is 2 Corinthians 12:10. Thank you from the bottom of my heart.

Lisa M., thank you for your references, Philippians 1:29

stays with me. I know that came from the Lord because that's not usually a comforting verse.

Mom, thank you for the email, and you sing "How great thou art" to your heart's content—I'll bring the hound dog in right on cue!

Love you all bunches, and I will have a good report tomorrow!

Friday, September 11, 2009, 12:36 pm, ET

Week 12, Friday prayer requests:

1. *Read Psalm 87*
2. *Continued strength through the journey*
3. *Remain infection-free*
4. *No reflux*
5. *No eye surgery*

Still refluxing

Noah had a great night! He did have an episode while I was holding him, but it was due to reflux, and we were able to stimulate him back without putting him back in the bed.

Even with going back to intestinal feeding, Noah is still refluxing, and it's just not as traumatic to his ability to breathe. They also started him on Maalox (an antacid) which seems to be giving him some relief.

Indy might be moving to a big girl bed today—a bassinet! I was so excited when I walked in yesterday and saw her in clothes and all wrapped up. Jenny, her mommy, said she was doing a good job holding her temperature. Indy is getting closer to going home too!

Thank you, Lord, for another day to worship you, experience your love, mercy, and grace, and witness your miracles. In everything, we give thanks.

Saturday, September 12, 2009, 10:47 am, ET

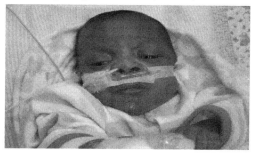

Waiting for him to find his voice

Yesterday was a much better day. Noah is still having episodes, but not as frequent or as bad. I believe once the reflux is taken care of, the episodes will stop.

Noah got a good scrub down last night and he did not like it at all. He just wiggled all around and cried. He still hasn't found his voice—when he cries there's no sound. He makes these faces that would make you believe he was being beaten or something terrible was happening to him—something besides water hitting his hiney! After the bath, he's quiet, content, and ready to go to sleep. Noah did stay up and visit with me for a while. We read our scripture and the Pajama Time book, and then we both went to sleep.

Indy moved to a big girl bed yesterday, and she's doing well. Remember her, Nyla, Phil, and the others in your prayers. I'm expecting a prosperous day tomorrow!

Week 13
Growth and boogies

Monday, September 14, 2009, 12:22 pm, ET

Week 13, Monday prayer requests:

1. *Read Psalm 90*
2. *Remain infection-free*
3. *No reflux/no surgery*
4. *No eye surgery*
5. *Good growth*

Car trouble doesn't even bother me
Noah is doing well; the last few days have been good days! He was circumcised yesterday-the nurse said he did really well and this is very good because he was temperamental earlier in the day. I'm not sure if he just didn't want to be bothered or he was adjusting to his new nurse-Noah likes to test the waters with new nurses, so he may have just been acting up.

We received some test results back that indicated Noah has a urinary tract infection (UTI), so he's getting treatment for that. The infection could be what was prompting some of the episodes last Wednesday. Now that he's circumcised, this should reduce the opportunity for infection. They'll repeat the UTI screen in a couple of days once he's healed from the circumcision. Noah has another eye exam this week, and we still believe he won't need eye surgery.

He get's nippled Maalox every six hours, and he's doing better with coordinating sucking, swallowing, and breathing while he's eating. They started giving him Pedialyte in a bottle, and only during the day shift while the doctors are there-this is written in his chart, to really work and give him a chance to get the coordination of eating by mouth.

I was having car trouble yesterday, but Noah had a good day, so it didn't bother me at all. More than anything else, I was worried I wouldn't get a chance to see him during the day.

The grandmother is back!

Yay for all of us! She and Noah had some quality time last night-I don't think she wanted to give him up and she's stuck on giving him sugar water. I'm going to have to do a thorough candy search before I leave Noah at her house. She's also making sure to tell him who's doing what to him. Noah has a way of pushing out his feeding tube (it's in his nose going to his intestines), and if it isn't in the right place, it can lead to problems. I kept telling mom to push the tube back in, and she wouldn't do it. So I did it, and she made sure to tell him that it wasn't her doing it, that it was his mom or his nurse. Mom, you are too funny!

Ready for Broadway

Noah was a show stopper during the day. When I got there, he was wide awake. Normally, once I hold him for a little bit, he drifts off to sleep, but not yesterday; he was up for almost an hour. Not only was he up, but he was following my voice, looking at me and making faces, and looking at the nurses and making faces. He even looked as if he were rooting-which he's been doing for a while now. I found it so funny because a couple of the nurses just couldn't believe how alert he was. Some were just amazed because they didn't think he'd come this far, or that the brain damage was so severe he wouldn't be able to do a lot of the things he's starting to do. The great thing about it is that they were so excited they'd go and tell another nurse, and another, and before you know it, half the crew had come by to see him. Important disclaimer; they never leave the other babies unattended, there's always at least one nurse in every room at all times. It makes my heart swell to see the love and interest they have for Noah, and I'm thankful to God for showing them another miracle.

I bought Noah a neat infant stimulating mobile (it should be neat after all the stores I visited trying to find one). You know, I'm learning that infant toy companies make toys more for the parents than the child. A lot of mobiles are designed to match the bedding or their room, but not for developmental purposes. I ended up getting him a cool mobile that he really enjoys-anything is better than looking at the ceiling, right? His day nurse asked him if he liked it right after I put it up, and he smiled right on cue!

Be prayerful for those kids going home and new ones coming in. I'm excited about our ice cream social we'll be doing this Thursday. I'm hoping more parents or grandparents come, but it will be just fine if it's just Jenny and me!

Check out Noah's mobile-it's the bright thing with the animals on it!

120

Monday, September 14, 2009, 9:14 pm, ET

Today's photo is of Noah's first bath in the tub. He looks like he enjoyed this one because he never opened his eyes.

We're episode-free so far today!

Noah had a very good day today. No episodes thus far; he drifted down a couple of times with his heart rate but no true episode. I met the speech therapist, and she was impressed with Noah's progress with the nipple. He can now take 5 ml. of Pedialyte twice a day. It sounds like such a small amount, but he's making progress. He's taking the Maalox down like a champ-it has a peppermint taste so that probably helps. Provided Noah doesn't have another infection, he can try taking milk from the bottle at the end of the week or the beginning of next week.

The doctor on this week is thinking the UTI is the reason for the last week's episodes, and the reflux was attributed to the infection as well. We can't say for sure, and we'll know how severe the reflux is when he starts taking feedings in his stomach again.

Our friend Leland went home today! Yay for Leland and

his parents. Leland was two months early (I think), and has been Noah's roommate for the last six weeks. As we say goodbye to him, we think we're one step closer to the day we get to go home too.

I had the privilege of going to Jenny's baby shower this past Saturday, and it was wonderful. I was so thankful and appreciative to put a face and give a hug to those who have been such an encouragement through the website. God bless you all and thank you for your prayers and continued support.
Meeting Tiffany was such a source of encouragement. Her little boy, Matthew, was also very premature and he's now a healthy two-year-old. Thank you, Tiffany, for reaching out and being a source of strength not just for Jenny, but for embracing me as well.

There's such a need for support or more resources for parents of preemies and Augusta, Georgia just doesn't have it yet. Hopefully, we can get something going that can fill the need. As Noah gets bigger and closer to going home, my heart aches for those moms who are coming in and delivering 2 and 3 months early; knowing their journey is just beginning. It is my heart's desire to be a support to them.

Wednesday, September 16, 2009, 11:15 pm, ET
Week 13, Wednesday prayer requests:

1. *Read Psalm 91*
2. *Remain infection-free*
3. *Tolerate feeds*

4. *Good report from all exams*
5. *Strength for mommy*

Noah has a packed calendar

Noah has had some good days, and this has been one of the busiest weeks I remember Noah having. He's doing great with taking Pedialyte from the bottle, as well as Maalox from the nipple. He's gotten A's from the nurses and speech therapist on his sucking and coordination. He had a cranial ultrasound yesterday morning, occupational therapy, speech therapy, and then a renal ultrasound late afternoon. He was recathed today to make sure he doesn't have any residual or new UTI.

Tomorrow he has a barium swallow test checking how he sucks, swallows, the path of the fluid, and if he has reflux. Then in the afternoon, he has another eye exam. He had another eye test scheduled, but it's on hold until next week.

Noah was episode-free for 24 hours the other day-I was thrilled! Since then, he's had a couple of episodes though, he self-recovered on a couple and needed major help on another. Noah is back to the contraption for his bottom. I'm praying he doesn't take after me with the skin sensitivities I have. I think his bottom problems are from having frequent stools, but I'm thinking the wipes could be contributing.

I am so ready to have Noah home-so ready!

Today marks 13 weeks of being in the hospital and pumping. I was at a point this weekend where I was just going to stop pumping and use the milk I've stored from the freezer. I wanted to get a few questions answered and some advice before I made a decision to stop though, so I called two contacts of prominent breastfeeding coalitions in our area on Saturday and have yet to hear back from either of them. I'm getting frustrated in reaching out to local organizations that pride themselves on their services, but seem to be all talk and no action. This is the second organization that hasn't responded. Do I have to become a stalker to get a response?

Dr. S and I talked about some of Noah's test results. I was less than thrilled about them, but am determined to avoid worrying about them. They are what they are and also the interpretation of the technician, but God has the final say. It's just one more thing to be able to laugh at the devil and give God all the glory.

Friday, September 18, 2009, 12:44 am, ET

Week 13, Friday prayer requests:

1. *Read Psalm 92*
2. *Wholeness for Indy*
3. *Remain infection-free*
4. *Tolerate feedings (bottle and stomach)*
5. *All babies and parents in the NICU*

Noah weighs 6 pounds-he's such a chunkster!

He's filling out so nicely and is so darn cute! I'm excited that I'm starting to see more of me in him as he gets older and plumps out.

Today was a pretty good day for Noah. He had the barium swallow test this morning, and he did very well. His nurse had everybody on their toes and assigned jobs when they got him down there. Noah has been known to show out a bit, all in his own timing, and we just weren't sure how he would tolerate the solution he had to swallow. Thankfully, he did the procedure with no problems. His day nurse said he actually liked the stuff and sucked it down without a problem.

Noah did show out a few hours later by having an ugly episode. He also had an eye exam late this afternoon and tolerated that well. I believe the doctor said he'd check Noah again in two weeks-this means his eyes have either stayed the same or have improved. Also, Noah might start having small amounts of milk to his stomach tomorrow!

Today was a good, but different kind of day. A baby was admitted to our room this afternoon, and sadly, unfortunately the baby didn't make it. My heart goes out to the baby's parents and the rest of the family for their loss. When I was able to go into the room and hold Noah, I just prayed for peace and comfort for the family and then thanked God for keeping and blessing me with Noah. I implore those with children to love on them as often as you can, regardless of their age. Kids are such a precious gift we often take for granted. I won't get on my soap box about that.

We had our second Parent Connect social tonight, and more people are coming out! We had two parents and two grandparents join the ice cream social. It's taking some time to grow, but I'm excited I'm not there by my-self anymore. I'm really looking forward to next month's meeting.

I'm very relieved Noah did well with his tests today-it's wonderful watching God move. I feel sad that Indy has to have another surgery in the morning. My prayer has been, and continues be, Lord, keep her healthy and strong.

I'm way too sleepy to type another word, and I'm about to pass out at the computer, so until next time.

Saturday, September 19, 2009, 1:04 pm, ET

Week 13, Saturday prayer requests:

1. *Read Psalm 93*
2. *Quick recovery for Indy*
3. *Tolerate feeding*
4. *Remain infection-free*
5. *Continued good growth*

He's gone more than 24 hours with no episodes!

Noah has had good days. He's back to getting feedings in his stomach, and has tolerated them well. He's had

126

minimal or no reflux. I've not seen him reflux, and none of the nurses have mentioned it either-we're making awesome progress!

As of yesterday, they're nippling Noah every other feeding. He gets 6 ml. of a mixture of Maalox and Pedialyte (sounds gross doesn't it?) and he's been getting it down great. They give him a little extra O2 support while nippling to help prevent any issues; it looks like it's helping so far. They've also increased the volume of his feedings to get back to full feeds in his tummy. As time progresses, the amount of the Maalox and Pedialyte mixture in the bottle should increase and then we'll eventually switch to milk in the bottle.

I got to bathe Noah again last night. He's just so funny to watch. His bottom is still open and sore but is getting better. The plastibell came off just fine and that area looks good. He still has swelling in his groin area, but nothing like it used to be. Noah now gets weighed twice a week because of his age and weight. His growth charts (weight gain and head circumference) are increasing the way they should, so a daily measurement isn't needed anymore. We still don't have a come home time frame, but I'm hoping it will be sometime in October.

Saturday, September 19, 2009, 7:19 pm, ET

The boogie monster

Today has been a good day! They are upping Noah's volume on his feedings and I think tomorrow they'll start condensing the running time from an hour to 45 minutes. This will help him prepare to take the bottle in his allotted 20 minutes. His nurse, said he did a good job with his coordination. It looked like he had things figured out-he has the sucking part down, sometimes gets a few reminders about swallowing, and he does good with breathing. The nurse said that sometimes babies forget the breathing part, but Noah stops to catch his breath and then continues.

His heart rate dropped a couple of times while I was holding him (before his feeding and bottle time), but we found the culprit-a big, thick boogie-GROSS! His nurse showed me how to do the bulb syringe (snot-sucker), and man did she hit gold on one nostril. It was a resilient boogie too, but Noah did much better after she got it out.

Yes, I know it's all a part of motherhood-boogies, poopies, and spit. I'll do it, but I didn't say I'd like it. I'm thankful for the bulb; there will be no sucking noses for me Auntie Judy. In fact, I may put a bulb and some bags in every room so I'm never caught without one.

Princess Indy is doing better, and she's making a speedy recovery. I was a little jealous when I saw her today lounging in her swing. Seriously, she is filling out so nicely and really looked so sweet and content in the swing. We have to work on getting Noah a swing or a bouncy seat-it's time to get him up and moving. Besides, I think he'll like it too, and it will give him a chance to move more freely and get out of the bed.

Week 14
Poopie prayers, bottles, and good days

Sunday, September 20, 2009, 11:57 pm, ET

Week 14, Sunday prayer requests:

1. *Read Psalm 96*
2. *Remain infection-free*
3. *For his bottom to heal quickly*
4. *Tolerate all feedings (stomach and bottle)*

One step closer at a time

Noah has had a good day. He made it all the way to 8:00 pm before having an episode today. It still sounds like he has a lot of snot up his nose which is more than likely contributing to the episodes. He's tolerating feedings to his tummy well, even with the condensed feeding time, he's getting a Pedialyte bottle with every feeding, and tomorrow they'll do two feedings with milk—they'll fill the bottle and let Noah drink as much as he wants, then do the rest via tube feeding. I'm so excited because this means we're one step closer to going home!

Noah's bottom is raw, and it's just awful. It wasn't as bad yesterday as it is today. We have to get it fixed, and quickly. It's like an adult having a bed sore; it's a site for infection. Not only that, but I know it's painful for him. He has another test, a VCUG—it checks the urine flow and bladder plumbing. He maintained his oxygen saturation level, and it was higher than his usual, normally he'd be set for 95 and was doing 99. They want to make sure everything is going the way it's supposed to, and the food isn't taking a wrong turn in there.

I gave Noah a bottle for the first time tonight; we both did very well! Noah maintained his levels and they were actually higher than they needed to be and he took all 5 ml. For the 9:00 pm bottle, he didn't want to wake up, so I couldn't force him to take it. However, he woke up a little later and I was able to give it to him.

Feeding a preemie is way different from feeding a newborn. He has to be sitting up and away from my body, and a finger or two goes under his chin for support, helping (reminding) him to swallow. I was so excited to be able to give him a bottle; it's just one more thing I can do to be a part of his care. I won't be able to give him a bottle with milk until the staff is sure he's comfortable with taking it (where he doesn't have any issues). I'm just delighted to be able to do more for, and with Noah.

Tuesday, September 22, 2009, 2:42 am, ET

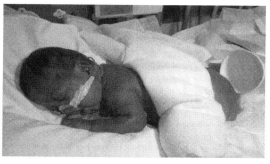

Week 14, Tuesday prayer requests:

1. *Read Psalm 97*
2. *Healing of bottom*
3. *Tolerate feedings*
4. *Wean from O2 support*

Noah had no episodes, and that's a blessing

Monday was a good day. They've had to increase O2 support occasionally when he'd get upset, but they've always been able to wean him back down. Noah's still on heated high flow, and we need to get to pediflow.

Noah had another eye exam today that caught us off guard. His eyes haven't gotten worse, and they haven't gotten better, so they'll get checked again next week. The VCUG (voiding and plumbing test) is postponed until Tuesday. We're keeping his bottom diaper-free and exposing it to O2 and the heat lamp to heal it. We're looking to start giving him milk in the bottle sometime this week. He's still getting the Maalox and Pedialyte mixture.

I am so proud of Noah's progress. He really is becoming a big boy in every way. His bottom is still taking a lot of work to clear up.

He is pooping more than ever! I think back to the time he was having a hard time going, and we were praying for him to poop—well, our poopie prayer was answered months ago, and it's still being manifested!

We're keeping his diaper open, so his bottom will heal quicker, and we'll have a better chance of seeing and smelling when he's made a stinky—which by the way, seems like it's never ending. Tonight, every time I changed him and put a clean diaper under him, he was going again or would go while I was putting it under him. He's well hydrated, and his poop has a good consistency. Anyway, that's enough about poop-talk for today.

He looked so cute when I saw him earlier today. I knew they were keeping the diaper open, but yesterday, he had t-shirts on to keep from getting cold. Well, today I was greeted with Noah in his birthday suit! It was the cutest picture to date. I ended up putting a hat and some socks on him to help keep some of his natural body heat in, but when I left we were down to just the hat—he kept peeing on his feet.

It's so time for Noah to come home

We have to master the feeding thing and get off of this O2 support. The two are intertwined and play off of each other. I had an enlightening conversation with the younger Dr. B tonight. I saw him when I came in and was going to ask him some questions, but figured I'd wait until tomorrow because it was so late. As I was in visiting with Noah and talking to a night nurse that's been with us since the beginning, young Dr. B walked in and just hung back listening to our conversation for a bit. I didn't realize he was waiting on me, but he jumped in to answer my questions. We touched on a few scenarios of getting Noah home and things to consider for the near future. Where's the easy button when you need it?

Lord, give me the wisdom to make the best decisions for Noah and clear eyes to see the way in which we should go.

Wednesday, September 23, 2009, 11:22 pm, ET

Week 14, Wednesday prayer requests:

1. *Read Psalm 98*
2. *Continued healing of his bottom*
3. *Remain infection-free*
4. *Swelling in his groin to go down*
5. *Continue tolerating feeds*
6. *Accelerated development*

Trying not to be selfish

Noah is doing well; he's had some good days. We were episode-free up until 10:45 pm. We discontinued antibiotics today; his nose hasn't been as runny as he was the past two days, his bottom is getting better, so prayerfully by the beginning of next week it will be completely healed. The VCUG (voiding and plumbing test) came back normal, he's taking the bottle pretty well and has learned how to pace himself, so he doesn't choke himself—thankfully he's not a spitter. Noah's groin is so swollen; I want to fuss. The area is so swollen we can't retract the foreskin to get to his penis. So, I'm praying there are no adverse effects.

We hit 14 weeks today! Noah has come a long way, and I'm so proud of him and all the progress he's made. I'm convinced he's ready to move forward with feedings, so I'll be working to get the doctors on board. I thought we were on the same page, but tonight demonstrated that we're not. It's funny (not really, but I do have to find the humor) to see and listen how people hear only the parts they want to hear. Someone told me they had been keeping up with Noah and his progress, yet didn't know that feeds were no longer going to his intestines, but back to his stomach. The part that was kept up with was my wanting more information about a g-tube. So, once again I say, I will not make a decision concerning Noah out of selfish reasons for me. Yes, I want him home, but I won't shortchange him or take any opportunity from him to do it on his own.

I'm told many times by many people that I need to take

a break from going to the hospital, stay home in the evening, or go away for a couple of days. All of that sounds fantastic, and I even consider it at times since I'd enjoy the getaway, but I just can't do it; my mind just won't let me. It's not that I don't believe he's in good hands; it just doesn't sit well with me not to be with Noah when I can. It's just not "normal" to be home without your baby. I enjoy the time I'm able to spend with him and learning how to care for him. This also lessens my learning curve for when we come home. I'm glad I have the availability and opportunity to go the way that I go, especially when there are hang ups.

Yesterday we had an ugly hang up, and I give praise and glory to God for keeping His hand on Noah. The oxygen was not hooked back to Noah after his respiratory therapy (RT) treatment. His nurse couldn't figure out why the oxygen saturation wasn't picking up; so she checked Noah and turned it up a bit. Now, he typically responds fairly quickly when it's turned up, but it was still reading, "dash, dash, dash."

I said, "He's breathing, he's not black, and he's not washed out." As I think about it now, he was a little pale, but nothing like he'd been in the past. I thought the monitor wasn't tracking because the sensor was on his arm and it can be tricky to get an accurate reading especially when he's moving around. Let me add that his heart rate had not dropped during this time. His nurse went to turn it up again, and at that point, we both realized something didn't look quite right. Then, we figured out his O2 line wasn't plugged in! And it's not like he was only without O2 support for 2-3 minutes, it was well over 10 minutes. So, to me, that's a case where I ask, "Would it have been caught if I wasn't there?" I'm sure they would have figured it out eventually, but at what expense? Furthermore, I believe if I hadn't been there, I wouldn't know that it had happened and that's what concerns me.

I know nobody's perfect and mistakes happen—but that was just unacceptable to me. I'm thankful that God gave me peace throughout the situation. I was upset, but I wasn't ugly, nor did I have a nasty tone in my voice when I talked with the therapist, nor did I think any ugly words (that is major growth for me and even more so because it involved my son).

Lord, thank you, thank you for keeping a hedge of protection around Noah and not letting any harm come to him. "No weapon formed against him shall prosper," Selah.

Friday, September 25, 2009, 10:21 am, ET

Week 14, Friday prayer requests:

1. *Read Psalm 99*
2. *Tolerate bottle feeds*
3. *Remain infection-free*
4. *Accelerated growth*
5. *Rest/peace/strength*

Music to my ears

Noah had a good day yesterday. He weighs 6 pounds, 5 ounces now! His bottom is getting better, it's still being exposed to the oxygen, but he has clothes on now. He's just about to outgrow the newborn diapers and hit size 1 diapers. He got to ride in the swing yesterday afternoon—unfortunately, I wasn't there to see him in it, but his nurse said he enjoyed it. He didn't know what to make of it at first, and his eyes were big and wide open. He wasn't fussy, he had his paci, and was taking in the sights until he went to sleep.

He's a little temperamental with taking his bottle; not that I can blame him because he may just not be hungry every time it comes around. He did well with his 3:00 am, 6:00 am, and 9:00 am feedings; the noon feeding took some work for him to drink it—he was just not waking up for it. So, when he's wide awake, feedings are no problem, waking him to eat takes a little labor.

He had a couple of episodes in the early morning. I was able to talk to the doctor about possibly breastfeeding, especially since they've increased the volume of his feedings (10 ml. in the bottle). The doctor was all for it and said, "If that will make you happy, go for it." This was music to my ears so today is the day we get to try it! I'm so excited and so glad I didn't stop pumping.

Thanks to Jenny for the note and the bags; it was a real pick me up! You know, you do something for so long and then it seems like what you're holding out for will never come. I guess this is an appropriate reminder for, "Don't be weary in well doing."

Friday, September 25, 2009, 10:22 am, ET

Today is going to get better

The plans to breastfeed are off for the day. I received a call from the doctor at 9:30 am telling me Noah spit (milk came up and out) and had to be bagged. He did say it was over as quickly as it started, but he doesn't want to stress him any further today. So, that means no more bottle feeding or anything else by mouth today. I'm contacting a surgeon to gather more information on a pH probe and the g-tube. I've not opted for the surgery at this point—I need more information before going that route.

Continuing to give God glory, working to keep a smile on my face, and get through yet another phase.

Week 15
Days of Our Lives with All our Children who might have One Life to Live at the Hospital (also, my boobs got some action)

Sunday, September 27, 2009, 2:08 am, ET

After 101 days of pumping and three code blues, we finally breastfed!

Grandpa Bill, you were right, the next day got much better. We got to breastfeed today! I am so excited and so thankful! Noah did an excellent job. He kept his heart rate up, his O2 levels were in the 90's to 100, plus the highest his respiration hit was 76, so he wasn't wearing himself out to suck. Noah could have been the "Got Milk?" poster child—except he had a milk goatee instead of a mustache. It took several minutes to get situated, and we ended up using a nipple shield, but we got it together, and Noah got some mommy milk! It was such a wonderful feeling and experience! Thank you, to our night nurse, for helping us, Dr. B for letting us try, Jenny for the encouragement, and great thanks to God for putting it all together!

Monday, September 28, 2009, 8:47 pm, ET

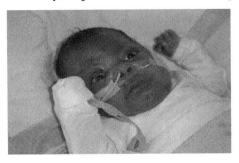

Week 15, Monday prayer requests:

1. *Read Psalm 103*
2. *Remain infection-free*
3. *Accelerated development*
4. *Continue good feeding/no reflux*

Breastfeeding is frustrating!

I don't have a new weight on Noah yet, but I think he's past his last weight of 6 pounds, 5 ounces. He's still filling out so nicely—his chubby cheeks and chunky legs are just too cute!

He was in his birthday suit warming his bottom when I saw him today. His bottom is healing nicely; there's just one stubborn spot that needs to heal. I'm praying it heals fast because it can be a source for other issues and it's keeping him bed-bound more than he needs to be.

Noah is now getting 15 ml. in a bottle and is taking it like a champ. When he finishes, he's always looking for more, but they're making us take it slow for his safety.

Still working on the groin area; it will get better once he gets off his stomach. He was virtually episode-free today; he just drifted a bit.

We're working the breastfeeding thing. I think I'm more frustrated than Noah is. It would be so much easier if I had more milk, but he's working with what I got. He has a great latch and suck (when he decides to suck). Tomorrow we get to learn infant massage... oooh aaaaahh.

Noah has done well with the bottle and breastfeeding; however, there's still a hint of reflux. I consulted with a surgeon today about the situation, and he thinks Noah could benefit from surgery. I'm not excited about the idea; however, I'll do whatever it takes to get Noah better and to get him home in the safest manner. The surgeon isn't rushing me, yet I know I need to make a decision, and sooner rather than later. I'm still looking for the ram in the bush and praying God will fix it.

We had such a great cuddle session today. We held each other skin-to-skin for four hours—oh, it was heavenly. We both took a nice nap, Noah ate, took a nap; ate again, and took another nap. He stayed up for a little while to chat with me and watch his mobile. He even gave me a few presents today; he almost got me the other day, though. I was changing him, looking at his bottom, and about to put some ointment on him when he let loose and squirted. I was able to get the diaper up enough, so it didn't get out of hand, but he managed to get it on the sheet and his blanket. I'm just thankful I moved my face when I did; I would not have been happy to have a poo face.

Muh got to feed Noah last night. I left early to let them do their grandma-grandson thing. She said he did a great job and sucked the milk down in no time, and wanted more! I'm so thankful to have the support that I do. It makes the process more bearable and helps to keep me sane.

We still don't know when Noah will be coming home—it most likely depends on surgery and recovery or how well he tolerates his feeds and can wean from O2 support. I do know I'm ready for Noah to come home. We've passed my due date; I'm beyond tired, and ready to not have to "visit" my baby anymore.

Wednesday, September 30, 2009, 1:36 am, ET

Week 15, Wednesday prayer requests:

1. *Read Psalm 104*
2. *Remain infection-free*
3. *Accelerated development*
4. *Indy to take the bottle*

Noah has hit 6 pounds, 9 ounces—my, how he has grown!

He's doing very well on the bottle; taking the 15 ml. easily and even drinks the little extra in there. He's really done a good job sucking, swallowing, and breathing and has learned how to pace himself well. He hasn't had any problems with choking or spitting while taking the bottle—that tends to happen a little later.

A wound care nurse looked at his bottom and prescribed an ointment which has made a difference just in the last 12 hours. Between Xenaderm and A&D ointments, and frequent changes we're getting the job done to heal his bottom.

Noah had 4 episodes today, 3 of which I was present, and were related to reflux. Thankfully, he didn't need bagging on any of them, but they're still scary and make my heart skip a beat.

We did infant massage this afternoon, but Noah wasn't feeling it. He was hungry, ready to eat before his scheduled time, and was not trying to hear, "Relax, calm down; this will make you feel better"; he had a one-track mind and let us all know about it.

Today was a different kind of day

I felt heavy for a good part of the day, even before getting to the hospital. The whole NICU is isolated, so everyone has to gown-up, and put on a mask and gloves before going into the room. At this point, no one is known to be infectious; however, it's possible that new moms may have had the flu. Having to put all this gear on makes our visits feel tedious. My heart was heavy in wanting to understand why God lets things happen the way they do. Not just with me, but with so many people. A friend of mine should have celebrated her soon-to-arrive grandson at a baby shower this past weekend, and instead, she attended his funeral. I just think of all the people who want children and can't have them, and then all the people who don't want or shouldn't have kids but end up as babymaking machines. I still trust Him, yet He knows I have major questions about these situations.

I decided for Noah to have the surgery

Making this decision made my heart feel heavy. I'm not worried about it working, or scared that I won't be able to take care him; I just don't want him to have to have surgery. I wanted to know in my heart of hearts that this is what he needs. I prayed for God to make what I need to do crystal clear, and based on the episodes today; I think I received my answer. I consulted with a nurse practitioner before the episodes, and she said many parents opt out of surgery and work to control the reflux with medicine, and it's not uncommon for them to have an episode at home and die. That isn't an option, and I will not put Noah at risk—he hasn't come this far to go out like that. We don't have a date at this point, but it should be within the next two weeks.

I don't want to leave this entry on a negative note. As I sat in church service tonight, I felt like Bishop was speaking directly to me. He said, "You may not know what the future holds, but you know who holds your hand through it," and, "God's best is yet to come." I'm holding onto God's word and promises and finding, "Joy through the Journey."

Thank you to Indy's grandma's coworker for the bib, it's precious and so thoughtful. I found out baby Phil is doing much better—his surgery went well, and he could very well be going home within two weeks. I'm so happy he's doing good, and even happier they'll be going home soon. Phil and his family have been on this journey since the end of May.

Wednesday, September 30, 2009, 11:55 pm, ET

Where are the days going?

It's about 12 weeks until Christmas, 8 before Thanksgiving, and 4 before Harvest (Halloween), and I'm trying to figure out where the time has gone. I'm also wondering how much longer we'll be in the hospital. I'm working on getting things lined up for this surgery and figuring out where he should have the surgery. I also just learned the nursery had been compromised with RSV and possibly the flu. The aggravating part is that I don't know which or how many rooms are affected. On top of all of that, I learned tonight that Noah has to have eye surgery. These are all the details I have, so I'm anxious to talk to the doctor in the morning.

It was a madhouse in there today. I don't think my heart dropped nor had my stomach cringed so much in a day. The code blue alarm went off several times during my visit with Noah. All I could do was pray for the babies and the parents. I was concerned when I learned what room the nurses were responding to because I know the parents of both babies in there.

People often have the misconception that once your baby is growing or has hit a certain weight, then you should be on your way home, or it's not as critical as a new arrival. As much as I'd like to convince myself of that, it's not the case. Some babies born early just need to eat and grow and then they can go home, and others have a different road to travel. Ours is the different road. Once he can eat, breathe, and hold his temperature, we can go home. So far we're at one and a half out of three.

Remember Indy, Nyla, baby Phil, and the other kids in the NICU in your prayers. Pray they all remain infection-free and go home healthy.

Lord, continue to keep our children and us. Strengthening all of us, mind, body, and soul. My prayer is for Your will to be done and that you get all of the glory from each of our situations. We need a breakthrough, a miracle that only You can create. Show me where to find comfort in Your Word, especially when I begin to doubt. In Christ's name, I pray, Amen.

Saturday, October 3, 2009, 1:14 am, ET

Week 15, Saturday prayer requests:

1. *Remain infection-free*
2. *Successful eye surgery*
3. *Successful bottle feeds*
4. *Mommy's strength and remain calm, cool, and collected*

Surgery time

Noah had a really good day on Thursday. I got him a bouncy seat, and his nurse said he really liked it. He was keeping her company in the wee hours of the morning, so she put him in it, turned on his mobile, and he was a happy camper. He was trying to catch (or dismember) the animals on his mobile. I really wish I could have seen that! He weighs in at 6 pounds, 10 ounces now.

The last two days have been unbelievable. Noah had an eye exam on Wednesday, and the result was him needing eye surgery. When the doctor told me he'd have surgery on Friday, I was totally not prepared to hear this. In trying to keep the reflux surgery (fundoplication and g-tube) in front of me, I say why not do both surgeries on the same day, so he only has to be intubated once?

Yes, it's possible but it's not where we are because they no longer do the reflux surgery at this hospital. I now wish I had been more persistent about seeing what the time frame would have been in going to other hospitals. The doctors wanted to go ahead and do Noah's eyes before they got any worse, so we did.

Noah had eye surgery at 2:00 pm on Friday and he did extremely well. The nurse who was with him said he had no problems; she was expecting the worst, but he was on his best behavior. He was weaned off the vent and had a little issue with it; he was having a hard time staying awake and was having episodes (dropping heart rate and O2 levels).

Noah was moved back to his room tonight and was able to take a bottle for his 9:00 pm feeding; he did an excellent job! He took the 20 ml. in about 10 minutes and probably could have had more. He also did well with his midnight feeding. I'm learning Noah can be an obstinate little boy, especially during feeding time. He's determined and strong-willed with keeping his mouth shut and not dropping his tongue. Mommy's learning some tricks to overcome his obstinance though. Noah also got the first of five Synagis shots; he'll get one a month for the next five months.

Seeing Noah before surgery was probably the second hardest thing I've had to do so far. Seeing him back on the ventilator, twitching a bit (they heavily sedated and partially paralyzed him), his eyes were wide open as if he was asking, "What's going on? Mommy, please help me!"—it was awful, just awful. After holding one of his hands and stroking his head, he went to sleep.

I had been fine up until that point, and after that, my nerves went way bad. This is the first time during this whole ordeal that I've had a major eczema flare up. Stress has been a major trigger for me in the past, yet I haven't had a bad reaction until today. While I was in the waiting room, my hands and parts of my arms became so swollen, red, hot, and itchy. Jenny told me to sit on my hands, but I told her then I'd look like I was scratching my butt. The eczema flare-up did come, but it didn't last past the time he got out of surgery. The surgery went very well, and Noah was recovering well. His eyes were nothing the way they described they would be. They said they'd be red, swollen, and would possibly have some bloody drainage—I'm thankful they didn't.

Coming off of the ventilator is a process and at times a tedious one. As Noah was coming off of the vent, he had several snags. His heart rate and O2 levels were dropping, and the staff was having a hard time getting them and keeping them up. They gave him something called Narcan, which helps to reverse the sedative and wake him up. They gave him a second dose of Narcan, and his nurse said if that didn't work, he'd have to go back on the ventilator because she needed to get caught up and didn't have time to stay back there with him.

On three separate occasions I had to step out of the isolation room where he was and into the main room to get someone to help me because I was having a hard time getting Noah to respond (I had to leave his room even though his monitor was to alert the main room). The last time I had to get someone, it was about time for me to leave because of shift change. Noah's monitor went off again while staff was there, so I went to see if I could hear it in the main room—and I couldn't. I went back to where Noah was and informed his nurse I wasn't comfortable leaving him in the isolation room when he'd be by himself and his monitor wasn't alarming in the other room.

This is when poo poo hit the fan

The nurse tried to reassure me the monitor was on, they could hear it, and they'd respond, but I wasn't convinced because I had to go get someone to help 3 separate times in 2 hours. The nurse and I go a couple of rounds about that.

Then, the staff decides that Noah will move back to the room he was in before surgery. That became a problem because the plan was to let the night shift staff move him back to his room, that way she could chart. Since

Noah had to have the eye surgery, they placed him on a different bed than his own, and the new bed he was on didn't stay inclined. To help his airway and reduce reflux, the nurses put several blankets under the mattress to prop him up. They decide to move him back to his bed in the other room, and for whatever reason, the nurse yanked the blankets from under him (he was being sat up on the bed by another nurse) and slammed them on the bed right next to him. I told her she could be mad, but not to take it out on Noah, and more poo hit the ceiling.

She proceeded to step towards me, get in my face, and start yelling

Oh Lord, thank you for restraining my tongue. Thank you, mother, for distracting me; the situation was going from bad to worse and about to get worser (I know that's not a word, but it fits for this situation). It's amazing (funnier to me now) that there were two more people with us in the isolation room, but they were like flies on a wall—they said absolutely nothing; there were nurses in the main room and no one that I can recall, came to help until his nurse went to chart and it was time to move Noah back. Needless to say, I was super pissed off and didn't leave until he was settled back in his room, in his bed. I was extremely thankful for the nurse he was transferred to that was able to get him situated and comfortable.

Now, I know everybody has a bad day or even a bad life going on; I have bad days too, but today was taken to a whole new level of unprofessionalism. I feel like I'm in a freakin' soap opera: Days of Our Lives with All our Children who might have One Life to Live at the Hospital. The saga and drama are as long as the title.

The moral of my story is, as Noah's mother, I'm his advocate. He's my responsibility, and his welfare is my first priority, and even through discourse, you can treat others the way you want to be treated. As I write this, I may not actually have a point, but it sounds good to me, and I feel better getting the encounter out of my head and onto the page.

Jenny, I will have my water balloon session this week. You're more than welcome to join me.

Week 16
Moving day

Sunday, October 4, 2009, 8:30 pm, ET

Yesterday was a much better day than Friday. I met with a supervisor and got some things cleared and straight. Noah's nurse today lobbied for him to be fed every four hours and to let him take however much he wanted from a bottle and then gavage (tube feed) the rest. He averaged 35 ml. and took 40 ml.—this is very exciting, 10 of which was medicine (yuck). In the wee hours of the morning, he took 50 of 70 ml. He had an episode, yet again related to reflux. I've noticed a bit of a pattern of when he'll reflux. To be continued...

Monday, October 5, 2009, 12:39 am, ET

Pray for what God lays on your heart and mind

Today has been a mix of emotions. Noah has been in episode city since about 2:00 pm. He's been doing really well with his bottles, but today he hasn't been himself.

He's been pretty irritable which isn't his temperament at all. They initially thought he had too much fluid on him since he hadn't received a dose of diuretics since Wednesday. I think it's an infection, maybe a UTI. He's exhibiting similar behavior as he did when he had a UTI last time. They said tonight his blood gas look good, so at this point, he didn't need to go back on any breathing assisted machine and his lungs looked and sounded clear so no need to resume CPT (beating that loosens fluid buildup) or the steroid treatment for his lungs. When I left, they were starting antibiotics just in case it was a UTI and decreasing the volume and frequency of his feedings. So, feedings are back to every three hours and about 55 ml. Prayerfully, we find out what it is quickly, and it's an easy fix.

I had the opportunity to participate in the hospital's annual Walk to Remember this afternoon in memory of Parks E. Schaffer. It was such a touching ceremony that allows parents to come together, grieve their loss with family and friends, honor and celebrate their child's life, leave their mark in the serenity garden, and continue to create precious memories in spite of their loss. I was blown away at the number of parents there who've lost their child many years ago, and then there were those who have lost more than one. I'm amazed by how they're still able to honor their child.

When a pregnancy doesn't take the "normal route" you're thrown into a whole new world. A world that many people are fortunate not to know about and don't understand. With that, many don't understand the life, the hardship, or the grief for those who do have to travel the hard road. There were some nuggets that I received just in going to support my friends.

1. **Grief is a relationship that's been broken.** In the first few days after having Noah, his nurse at the time told me, "Naomi, you have to grieve what you thought your pregnancy would be and then you will heal and be able to handle this journey." It made sense when she said it, and it became clearer for me today. Grieving what I expected to happen: seeing my belly get big, taking maternity photos, having a natural delivery, which I'll never be able to do with a subsequent pregnancy, my baby and me going home together, seeing, touching, holding, and kissing him whenever I wanted. Yes, Noah is still here, and I'm so thankful for that, yet there's still a grieving process in motion.

2. **Grief is a process and not a product.** It can't be rushed or put on someone else's timetable. So many times I don't grieve when it's most needed, thinking I'm weak, or so much time has passed, and I should be over it by now. I'm not saying this to stay and wallow in it, but the process isn't something that goes away in a couple of days, or weeks, or even months. I still find myself grieving my expectations and most days are better than others. But God is showing me, and I confirmed it yet again today, that through this situation He will get the glory and I've been chosen to handle this mission for His purpose. This isn't about me. As much as think it should be or want it to be it's all about the sovereignty of God.

I got to officially meet Grandpa Bill (Indy's granddad). I've only seen him once before, on a Friday night (when I first met Jenny) and he offered to make some root beer floats for my mom and I as we were all sitting in the family waiting room. I appreciate your prayers and words of encouragement, and now I know where Jenny gets her silliness.

Noah was actually able to gift some of his clothes already. We gave Broderick, a new baby to the NICU, a cute bear sleeper and some onesies that Noah never wore. We're growing and on our way home.

Tuesday, October 6, 2009, 12:39 pm, ET

Week 16, Tuesday prayer requests:

1. *Pray Psalm 109*
2. *Infection to clear quickly*
3. *No more infections*
4. *Wean off the ventilator*
5. *Strength*

The past 30 hours have been rough, very rough

Noah was placed back on the ventilator early Monday morning, around 3:00 am. He had an infection grow out from the blood culture and just found out another grew out from the urine culture, the RSV test was negative, he's fairly stable, he's on a fair O2 setting, but is getting a lot of support from the ventilator. He had been rid-ing the vent a good bit yesterday and letting it do a lot of breathing for him, but he did have periods where he breathed well over it. His bottom looks much better than it has. I'm prayerful it continues to get better. The antibiotics are making his stools loose which causes his skin to breakdown. Noah is still getting his feedings through the feeding tube. He isn't tolerating being touched at all. Changing his diaper has been a chore because he'll just bottom out.

Noah's eyes seem to be doing well. He's been up following his mobile at times, and he'd follow my voice a bit. I'm not sure when the doctor comes back to check them; it should be sometime this week. I hope the latter part of the week. Otherwise, I'm not sure how he'll handle the procedure.

...

I'm so full of emotions I don't know where to begin. At times, I feel that because I ask so many questions, some think I'm questioning their nursing ability which isn't where I'm coming from at all. I ask questions because that's who I am and how I learn; I like to know how things work, what's being done, and learn how to take care of my son. I'm thankful and grateful for those who take the time to incorporate me into Noah's care. I want to make the load easier for them and not harder. The more I can do for him, the more time they can spend providing care to another baby.

This roller coaster ride is wearisome

Outside of the physical part (that's the easy part), the mental and emotional parts are butt-kickers. I'm working really hard to stay encouraged, and reminding myself this is just temporary, and it won't be like this forever—I tell Noah these things too. If I tell him these things, then I need to believe them. Again, my timetable isn't God's timetable, so I'm working to keep myself in His peace and in His rest. I shared with someone the other day that I now have a better understanding of David's writings of the Psalms. It was hard for me to grasp how in one Psalm he's so uplifted and the very next he's so downtrodden; now, I have more insight.

"Finding joy and strength from the joy of the Lord, knowing that's where my help comes from. Faithing Him through this process", and hopefully being a help to someone else along the way." (Hebrews 11:1)

Turning this pressure and what feels like and could be darkness into praise, deepening my relationship with Christ, and daily, finding joy through the journey. Without Noah and this process, I wouldn't have met the people that I've come to call friends. I'm grateful for the ever-expanding circle.

Indy has moved to the children's hospital across the street, so we're missing them. I believe everything will go smoothly, and this is one step closer to her being able to go home. Although we miss them already, I'm sure we'll see them very soon.

Wednesday, October 7, 2009, 2:27 am, ET

Noah has had a much better day today

They confirmed an enterococcus strain of bacteria in his urine, which had also gotten into his bloodstream, meaning he had urosepsis. They started him on a third antibiotic as well as Tylenol. The Tylenol is helping a great deal. Noah isn't as sensitive to touch now; he's working to get the tube out of his throat as often as he can; he's not succeeded yet—give him time, and I'm sure he will.

We're still scheduled for surgery on Monday. The doctors feel this is a good time to do it since he'll be finishing the course of antibiotics and should be healthy. At this point, I'm kind of praying he stays on the vent until after the surgery. I'd just hate for them to take him off and then a day or so later put him back on it due to the surgery. Either way, God has it worked out already. Noah hasn't had to stop eating! He's still getting fed every three hours and isn't missing a beat—Keep up the good work baby!

Mixed emotions about saying goodbye

I've started my, "see you later" talks with our nurses. For the last four months, I've always envisioned our farewells as happy times because we'd be going home; never did I think they'd be because we had to go to another hospital. Going to another hospital wasn't in my plans, but I'm not steering the ship. I feel so cheated from the "walk of fame" down the hall we would have normally made, stopping at the doors of each room and saying good-bye to all our new friends (doctors, nurses, therapists, parents, and babies). But for now, the walk will be done with a transport team taking us on another, extended journey.

Tonight was the last night we'd have one of our favorite night nurses. Thanks for all you've done; this isn't goodbye, it's, "See you later." You've been there since the beginning, and you allowed me so many firsts. We've laughed and cried together, and I thank God for bringing you into our lives. You're definitely an angel sent from above to care for us. May God pour back into you all that you pour out.

Thursday, October 8, 2009, 12:32 am, ET

Week 16, Thursday prayer requests:

1. *Pray Psalm 112*
2. *Restful sleep*
3. *Infection-free*
4. *Good transition*

16 weeks and counting

Each day is getting better and better. It's been 16 weeks since my perfect little angel Noah, was born. He's made such remarkable strides and has hit some great milestones. Even though he's still on the vent due to infections, he's getting stronger, and acting more like himself every day. He let me hold him for over an hour today which was heavenly! He was wide awake when I got to the hospital, and as soon as he got settled in my arms, he went to sleep; a deep sleep.

I received one of my last pieces of advice from Dr. S earlier today; he advised me to get some sleep and some good rest. This has been and still is a long journey, and I need to be on my A-game for Noah. Since we'll be moving to another hospital, I'll expend a lot of energy just communicating and learning a new system. So, that's my task for tonight; get eight hours of sleep (wish me luck!) I haven't slept eight straight hours without medicine since before I was pregnant, and I'm constantly reminded that I won't get that much of sleep for many, many years to come.

Noah's primary nurse was back today, and we're so happy to have her back. I'm going to miss her so much. She got Noah a University of South Carolina, Gamecock stuffed animal; she's going to start a rival with the rest of the family, but we don't mind—it was such a sweet gesture. Thank you for taking us under your wing, and caring for the both of us the way you have the past few months. You're always in my thoughts and prayers.

Noah's bottom is looking bad again—this is exactly what I was trying to prevent and wanted to create a course of action in case it did happen again. I'll talk to the wound care nurse again tomorrow, and hopefully, we can work out a regimen. I felt because we were leaving and his bottom was getting better they weren't really hearing my question. More so, since we're leaving, the new hospital will have their own groups and own treatment to handle the problem. I'm wondering what we do in the meantime to get it back on track. Once he has surgery, he won't be able to go on his belly and have his bottom open as he has in the past. Ugh! Sometimes I feel like I'm talking just to hear myself talk.

I'm not sure what's going on with Noah's feedings. We had to stop his 6:00 pm feeding because he was spitting, this is so not like him. He has also had way too much leftover after two of his feedings (25 ml. and 20 ml.); that's almost half of what went in. They decided to decrease the amount of fluid, and lengthen the amount of time that it takes to go in.

Noah made the news!

Noah made his first TV appearance today! We did an interview with Katie Beasley from WRDW, Channel 12 on the flu, H1N1, and precautions. It was the headline story on the 11:00 pm news and will be published on their website. It was great timing because the NICU just came off of a seven-day isolation, entailing gowns, gloves, and masks, every day, and for every visit. I took basic precautions and made the interview team wash their hands for three minutes and wear masks; even though they weren't going to be touching Noah.

Noah did a great job! He was wide awake, looking around, watching his mobile—you know, being Noah. Katie got sucked into Noah's world for a minute too.

She took her footage, packed up her equipment, and was getting ready to go, and since Noah was so alert, I turned on his mobile. She took the camera back out and taped this part as well, and it ended up being the main footage she used during the segment.

Noah is a ham already! He cut up right before the footage—he had to have another IV started because the other started leaking, he got the ventilator tube loose and had to have it re-taped, and then right after they left, he started to spit. He was perfectly fine during the taping! I hope people take precautions given especially when they're around babies.

An aside—I still have milk. I haven't pumped for several days, and my supply was about nil when I stopped. But now that I'm not thinking about pumping or breastfeeding—here it is! How rude!

Saturday, October 10, 2009, 12:01 am, ET

Noah has hit 7 pounds!

My chunky little boy; my how far we've come. I'm so thankful and grateful. We said our "see you laters" to the staff Thursday night and Friday morning. We had fun cutting up, and Noah stayed up the longest I've seen him yet; two hours. He was wide-eyed and wide awake and didn't have any episodes last night.

We've moved to a new location with new sights, new people, and a new system. Have I mentioned I'm so ready to get Noah home and get off this ride? We were supposed to leave at 8:00 am yet we got bumped twice and didn't leave until after 4:00 pm. By the time I was able to go and see Noah, I had 10 minutes to visit, most of which I spent answering demographic questions— questions that could have been answered by reviewing his records.

Seeing Noah tonight just broke my heart

His heart rate was higher than I've ever seen it, between the 170s-190s. Because the staff was about to have a shift change, I wasn't able to calm him, and he had nothing familiar to him. When I was able to go back in, I calmed him down. Noah introduced himself only as he could to the day nurse by bottoming all the way out. She mentioned she'd been warned about it, but wasn't really expecting him to do it—I promise we don't say things just to hear ourselves talk.

I'm working on keeping a positive attitude. I'm thinking last Friday was preparing me for our transition. Since Noah is on a ventilator, it's up to the comfort level of his nurse of whether I can hold him or not. We're in an isolation room because we're a transfer, so that means we have to gown and glove-up before we can go into the room.

I asked the night nurse where his monitor would ding and register since we're in isolation. She showed me where and informed me that all their kids show up and sound on this particular monitor. I promise not even five minutes after that conversation, Noah had an episode. I'm watching his heart rate sit at 0, and his oxygen sats drift down. I'm looking out in the room to see if anyone is coming to check on him, I'm checking his monitor, looking at Noah, back to the big room where the nurses and other parents are. I see the nurse who has Noah all the way across the room talking to the parents of another baby. So yet again, no one came to his room until I asked someone. I want to scream so badly! Seriously, am I asking too much to make sure isolation monitors pull up? I think not, but it's not looking that way. Then, not only were Noah's hands covered, they were tucked and bound under a blanket (granted it was to keep him from pulling the tube out, but to me, they could have used the mittens on his gown and then he wouldn't be able to get a hold of the tube and pull). I understand it would be bad if he pulled it out; however, he's a bigger, active baby. He has nothing to look at, listen to, nor can he stretch. It just puts me in the mind of Sea Biscuit (from the movie). I may be a bit extreme, but that's how I feel right now. Noah's old enough to know that his environment has changed, and I don't want his spirit to break.

To end this on a positive note, the good things that happened today were: Noah was transferred without incidence, I found some money in my bag, Muh got him a sound sleeper, he's tolerating his feedings, and we have a window in the room so now he can experience night and day.

I'm expecting tomorrow to be a better day and to be in this place a short, very short time.

Week 17
The champ of bends in the road

Sunday, October 11, 2009, 8:19 am, ET

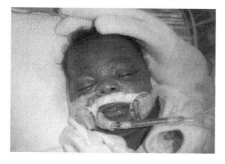

Week 17, Sunday prayer requests:

1. Remain infection-free
2. Good results from eye exam on Monday
3. Concerning surgery on Tuesday

Always adjusting

Noah is 7 pounds, 2 ounces and doing well. They had to restart his IV—it took three sticks, but they got it; he did great through that too. I'm very impressed with how well he's doing. I'm not sure if Noah's become immune to the sticking, prodding, and probing or what, but he's handling it like a champ. His bottom is looking better every day; he started on Aquaphor with a powder mixed in, and from what I can see it has helped a lot. Noah has an eye exam on Monday and another barium swallow test. He's still on the vent and won't come off until after surgery—I'm hoping I can talk to the doctor about that today. He still has gobs of secretions constantly coming out of his mouth (basically, it looks like he's foaming at the mouth), but that should clear when he comes off the vent.

Mommy is still adjusting to the new environment, but my disposition is better. We're on the "get a new nurse every shift" train. I've decided to make little notes from Noah for the staff (i.e. I like it when you talk to me, and mommy likes to change my diaper and bathe me.) I continually remind myself this is a very temporary stop; the stop we need to get us home.

Off to the hospital... until next time.

Sunday, October 11, 2009, 11:30 pm, ET
Week 17, Sunday prayer requests:

1. *Peaceful night and restful sleep*
2. *Remain infection-free*
3. *Good results from tomorrow's eye exam*

Expecting great things

Noah lost a little weight; he's back down to 7 pounds.
He's had a pretty good day today. He's off all medicines
except iron and the one for his liver. We liked our nurse
and respiratory therapist today. They're both very per-
sonable and talk to Noah when they work with him.
The nurses tell me he spent most of the day sleeping; I
haven't been there yet when he's been awake, except for
the first day. I went this morning and this afternoon, and
he peeked at me both times.

He did do a massive throw up job while we were holding. He had just settled in my arms when the nurse
stepped out of the room for just a few minutes, and he
just spewed like a volcano. I could tell he was a little
irritable, but I thought it was due to the vent tube and/
or because of all the secretions. Little did I know, he
was bringing up his 3:00 pm feeding. Well, the positive
that came from the volcano vomit was that I was able to
bathe him. He got a nice scrub down, lotioned up, got a
fresh set of PJs, and then spit up some more. The last one
didn't warrant changing him, but we did have to change
one of his sheets. We're not sure what caused the erup-
tion, but I'll be just fine if that doesn't happen again (at
least not that volume of vomit anyway).

I'm still working on getting Noah an identifying name
card. I've had the conversation twice with two different
people, and we still don't have one. It's not a big deal, but
it would be nice, and possibly helpful to others, to know
who's in that bed space. When he was transferred he
came in as, "baby boy Williams."

Hello! My name is Noah Samuel Williams & I'm 4 months old (DOB 6/17). I'm a happy baby & LOVE for you to talk to me when you Change me, Feed me, Bathe me, Stick me, etc. Thank you, Noah :)

Anywho, tomorrow is another day, and we're expecting great things. We miss our nurses and other friends—the parents and babies from our old hospital, but we're glad to be closer to going home. Still lifting them up in our prayers and praying for those in our new spot. Again, there are some who have been going through this longer than us—some as close to a year, and my heart goes out to them. I would like to meet them though because I'm sure they have a story to tell.

Mr. Broderick, our former roommate, gave Noah a parting outfit yesterday. I can't wait to see Broderick, Taylor, and Nyla again; to see how big they've gotten and what wonderful things they're doing.

I'm attempting to cross stitch; this should be an interesting project—I'm attempting this for Noah; we'll see if I have the patience to complete it; besides the fact, it's like reading Greek.
Until next time...

Monday, October 12, 2009, 11:55 pm, ET

Noah looks like a mummy in this picture—it looked like a jam-up tape job.

Week 17, Monday prayer requests:

1. *Accelerated development*
2. *Remain infection-free*
3. *Come home soon, healthy, and whole*

They canceled surgery!

Noah had a full day. He had an eye exam this morning and an upper GI. We don't have the results from the eye exam yet, but the upper GI showed that he's not refluxing (at least not in the three minutes they watched it). He had a chest x-ray, an EKG, an ultrasound of his testicles, a physical by the surgeon, and another by the neonatologist. He self-extubated and got a bath. Tomorrow sounds full as well. He has an EEG and cranial ultrasound scheduled and some other things that I think I've forgotten. Through it all Noah hasn't stopped eating; he's making sure he gets his groceries—that's my boy!

We met a nice nurse in the unit today; she reminds me of the nurses that befriended me at the other hospital. I didn't have very long to talk to her but could tell she has a sweet spirit. The nurse Noah had today was nice as well. I talked with the attending physician, and he's scheduled a family consultation later in the week. He puts me in the mind of Dr. S, just 10 times blunter.

They planned to keep Noah on the vent for a few more days until things got sorted out. The tube had just been re-taped early in the morning during the night shift. I left at 7:00 pm; Noah was sleeping, but still fussing with, and about the tube. I got back at 8:30 pm and they told me he had been a bad boy. His nurse said he had taken his tube out. I thought she meant his feeding tube; then it dawned on me she meant that he got the vent tube out! So, they gave him a chance on the nasal cannula, and he's been doing great! He's on 1 liter and 100 percent, sating 100 when I left.

I'm so proud of Noah. He never ceases to amaze me. Whenever I start feeling down or that we've lost ground, he and God do something new that puts a smile on my face and lifts my spirits.

Tuesday, October 13, 2009, 10:50 pm, ET

We finally came off of isolation and got a crib!

This is a monster crib! It is soooo big it's funny, but I'm thankful for it. I put Noah's mobile up, so he'll have something to look at and took his bouncy seat back tonight. Hopefully, he can get in it tomorrow.

Today was another busy day; lots of people from different departments and lots of tests. Noah had been episode-free up until 8:45 pm. The nurse said she wouldn't have known that he did anything if it hadn't been for the monitor. She was in the middle of her assessment, he was looking at her, then he closed his eyes, and his heart rate was at 0 (with a spaced out pattern), and the next thing she knows, he's back to 108. She said the day shift nurse had warned her, but she just couldn't fathom a baby doing that. Well, she got to see it firsthand.

They've weaned him down to 1/8 liter on the nasal cannula. They actually got him down to 1/16, but he wasn't tolerating that for too long. He's done well with his feedings, and we're still working on his bottom. He had a CT done this afternoon, and it took longer to get him ready to go and get down there than it did for them to do the test. Noah also had another echocardiogram today. I liked the tech that did it. She was very nice and explained what we were looking at on the screen. Needless to say, Noah slept through the whole thing. The heart doctor gave me the results—nothing is wrong with Noah's heart, everything looks fine, it's pumping, and blood is flowing correctly. This is great news and also not a contributing factor to the sudden and dramatic episodes. His eye exam results didn't show anything specific. They'll be back in a week to re-evaluate.

I talked to baby Phil's mom today, and he's doing well. He's home, and they're still transitioning. I hope I can see them before the week is out. Indy is doing fine. I've not seen her since we've moved, but her mom keeps me up to date. There's a baby in our room I've never seen, and know nothing about other than he/she cries all day. My heart goes out to that baby and continues to be in my prayers. Praying for a peaceful and restful night for all of the babies in both hospitals.

Thursday, October 15, 2009, 11:43 pm, ET

Week 17, Thursday prayer requests:

1. *Read Psalm 119*
2. *Restoration and complete wholeness from head to toe*
3. *Abundant life*

Mommy has had a tough, emotional day

Noah is 7 pounds, 5 ounces and doing well. He's tolerating his food and looking for his bottle. Still no time frame of when he's coming home, but there have been some conversations about it, maybe in November.

There've been no episodes for two days now, and that's good. They started Noah on a medicine that affects the vagus nerve, so between coming off the vent, and adding medication, it's helping control the episodes. His eyes are good and will be checked next week; speech and physical therapy consults should be next week as well. Noah's such a happy baby and making progress! He's getting better every day.

Today ranks up there with being asked to sign a DNR some weeks back. The doctor hit me with some dismal news. We have some massive challenges ahead of us and unfathomable mountains to climb, but we'll meet each one with grace, mercy, steadfastness, and God's unfailing love.

I learned some new things yesterday about Noah's delivery and the lengths that were taken to give him a chance at life, and I'm thankful. I think of the scripture in Jeremiah 1 where it says, "God knew you before you were formed in your mother's womb" (and that goes for each of us), and, "He knows the end from the beginning, and He has a plan for our lives, not of evil, but hope and an expected end."

As I think of those scriptures, I ask God, why would you allow this? Why would you do it this way? Help me see and feel you in and through this. Then I think of Jesus' words when He was in the garden and asked God if there was another way besides dying, and He came to the point and said, "Not my will but your will be done." God, you know, you know this is not the road that I would have selected for my life, nor my son's life, yet your will be done. Give me peace and rest through this journey. And to always be able to see the joy or the good in this journey. That I learn the lessons before me in this season of my life. And through this that you get all the glory. I'm reminded that we're made in Your image and are the likeness of You. I faith you with all that I am, my very being. I faith you with Noah and all that concerns him. I faith you with my finances. I faith you with all that concerns me. When I can't track you, I still trust you.

I've been reading these books by Karen Kingsbury, and they've been so timely. Although fictional, each book has had a way of speaking to me where I am. In reading today, there were several scriptures that came up and it was all I could do not to cry. I'm wondering, God, how can I say, "And I know that all things work together for good?" *(Romans 8:28) "How can I say and believe that when everything around me says different? And it comes back to trust and faith. Faith is the substance of things hoped for the evidence of things not seen." (Hebrews 11:1)*

Change is hard

I had a conversation with one of the doctors last week, and he was mentioning how momma's attitudes tend to change when they get here from another hospital. I couldn't quite understand what he meant by that, but after being there for a week I now know why they may change. I can't speak for other moms, but I can speak from my experience thus far. It's hard transferring to a new system; not only is it hard, but it's also stressful. I've spent four months in a place, learned the system, learned the environment, learned the people, and forged relationships and friendships. Uprooting is difficult in itself, and then having to go through a plethora of new people and a complex system is tiresome. I don't make excuses for any bad behavior, but I understand about being short, curt, and not always pleasant. I find it extremely taxing to have a host of people come to the bed, some introduce themselves and others don't. Some days I just want a timeout. Now some may think I'm complaining and others may think I don't understand, or say it doesn't work like that or whatever else might come to mind. But I say, why can't it work like that? It's called manners or etiquette. I don't have to be friends with you, I don't have to like you, and you don't have to like me, I'm not there to interfere with your job or your learning; however, as a patient and person, I expect to be treated as such and not a subject. I so want to go back into my pink bubble; I liked the world much better from there.

Speaking and sending life to Mommy, Daddy, Noah, Muh and the rest of the family as we travel through yet another bend in the road. Thankful for all of the prayers and words of encouragement. They truly bring tears of joy.

Friday, October 16, 2009, 6:12 pm, ET

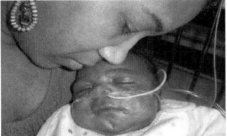

Week 17, Friday prayer requests:

1. *Read Psalm 120*
2. *Remain infection-free*
3. *Complete healing*
4. *Come home soon and completely whole*

Decisions, decisions

Noah has had a good day. He did well with speech therapy; they approved Noah to get a bottle on Monday with the speech lady. Soon, he'll likely have a modified barium swallow. The physical therapy tech came right after the speech lady and stayed for a long time. She gave me some suggestions on how to straighten Noah's legs when doing his exercises, and for when he's lying in bed.

Our pastors came by to see and pray over Noah today—this was a special treat for everyone. Noah actually opened his eyes for a little bit while they were there. He did have an episode this morning, I'm not sure if it was a full episode, but his heart rate dropped into the 60s; he did it again with me once.

We have some decisions to make next week regarding procedures, and I'm glad we have the doctor we have. He said when doing things you can't always make things right or better, but you definitely can make things worse, so there's no need to rush anything. We'll see what Noah needs now and work from there.

Noah and I had such a good visit earlier. We read one of our favorite books; "Do I Look Good in Color?" He stayed up through almost the whole thing! He would look from me to the book, and back again.

God was so sweet to me last night as I was going to sleep. After the day we had, all I wanted to do was crawl into the bed and sleep. I turned on the TV, and a preacher was teaching on Noah's characteristics. All I remember is him saying, "God will give you what you need to get through the floods of your life and that Noah meant peace, comfort and had grace and favor with God." He kept referencing the last part. I remember thanking God for being mindful of me and reminding me of His word and that He is mindful of Noah. That was just so sweet and comforting to my soul and spirit as I fell asleep.

Last night was the first night in a long while that I slept through the night and woke up rested and refreshed. There's a song that has resonated in my spirit for a while now by Twila Paris called, "Do I Trust Lord?" Some say it's a simple song, but it speaks volumes.

I'm off to bathe Noah and get my sugar and Noah fix!

Week 18
Seasons of big thinking

Sunday, October 18, 2009, 10:16 am, ET

My, how Noah is growing up

I gave him a bath on Saturday, and that was the first time he didn't cry or fuss through it. So now maybe it will be several years before he gets into that bigger boy stage of not wanting to get in the tub. The nurse said he didn't cry last night either when she bathed him.

Noah is letting us know he's very ready for his bottle; he's been pulling out the feeding tube more often—he pulled it out last night (maybe even twice), and I think he did it a couple of times earlier in the week. Thankfully, he gets to start on the bottle Monday; it will only be one time and probably not the whole thing, but it's a start. It's been two weeks since he's had one.

We like the nurse we've had for the last couple of days. She volunteers all the information that I'd normally have to ask about—that is so nice! She's way sweet to Noah too.

We're making progress and getting better every day!

Sunday, October 18, 2009, 9:54 pm, ET

Week 18, Sunday prayer requests:

1. *Read Psalm 123 and 124 (tomorrow's Psalm)*
2. *Remain infection-free*
3. *Complete healing and wholeness*
4. *Accelerated development*
5. *Good eye exam and report*
6. *Shock their socks off (in a good way) taking a bottle*

We continue to have good days—I don't expect anything less!

Noah's weight tonight was 7 pounds, 11 ounces! He's still holding onto fluid, but not a whole lot. He hasn't had diuretics since being at the new hospital. Noah's making progress with the oxygen support too; he goes between 1/8 and 1/16 of liter flow which is great. He was on 1/16 for two hours today which is a step in the right direction. He only did it for 30 seconds yesterday, so I'm happy with the improvement. Some think it's a small step, but I say—it's a step. They've upped his amount of food to 60 ml. and he handled it well. Tomorrow is the big day with the bottle—I think he's ready for it!

There's talk of coming home. Not a date, but the staff is mentally preparing me to bring Noah home. If he didn't have to have surgery, he would have been coming home. So, once the surgeries are knocked out, he's recovered, and I've received my training, then we can kick bricks (leave the hospital) and go home.

Noah is getting better every day and will not just have life, but an abundant one.

Oh my, I am so thankful to God. As I talked to Noah's nurse today, she told me how things went with this new technique in working with Noah's legs. She mentioned she tried it, but she didn't really notice Noah pulling his legs up to his chest. So, me being me, I pulled up his gown to look at his legs, and they were nearly straight out in front of him! I told her that his legs have never been this straight (I now stand corrected after looking back at earlier photos; his legs were straight for a little while after he was born, but for the past couple of months he's kept them pulled up). Some may not understand, and some may not believe it, but I don't care. It's significant progress!

At times I think God takes a break (I don't really think that, but it does feel like it sometimes) when nothing seems to be happening or moving on your behalf. Again, I say when I can't track Him I trust Him.

A sweet friend called while I was waiting to go back and give Noah his bath, and she just shared some of her heart with me. She told me how she saw God work and do things in His timing, even yesterday. As she traveled up the mountain and witnessed the seasons change—it was raining, and the leaves had changed some colors, but the further up the mountain she went, the more majestic the colors were, and it was snowing! How awesome it must have been to travel the same road, not at the beginning of the trip and not quite reach the end of it, but to have such a picturesque experience traveling from one point to the next. The moral of her story (and mine) is, God is in control, and He works on His timeline, not ours.

Fall is my favorite time of year because of the color changes, yet I'm fascinated by nature in general. Being out and observing nature in various environments lets me appreciate God. It's amazing how simple things seem, yet they're truly complex. I feel as if I'm babbling now—I say this to show that I'm encouraged!

Another thing to release; it's been running through my mind and pulling on my heart for a few days now. The staff mentioned on different occasions that I (and possibly a few other moms of babies with a similar history as Noah's) am in denial of what his outcome and quality of life will be. I've heard the worst case scenario, and I've heard the best cases in which have happened—that which medicine can't explain how or why they've done as well as they have. My response to those who say I'm in denial—I'm a big thinker and believer. For the record, those who know me, know that wasn't my first response—I plan to read this entire story to Noah as he gets older, and there are certain phrases I prefer for him not to learn from his mother.

You know, what you think and speak is what you bring to life—a good book to read on this topic is, "Commanding Your Morning" by Cindy Trimm. If I'm going to spend time thinking, talking, and wondering about the future and all the unknowns, then they're going to be positive thoughts.

Only God knows how everything will turn out. I'm confident those who have children do everything in their power to keep their child from being labeled or wrongfully grouped. I'm no different. Noah is able and capable of having a productive life. I believe people reach for what's expected of them, especially children.

I remember when it was time for me to move up to high school, and the middle school teacher had to recommend us for the college prep track. My teacher told me she wasn't going to recommend me because she didn't think I had what it took to be on that track, so she recommended me for the general track. I wasn't a bad student nor did I perform poorly; yes, I had my challenge subjects, but what kid doesn't?

Had it not been for my mother pushing and advocating for me, who knows where I would've ended up. She believed in me, knew what I was capable of, and wasn't going to settle for anything less. To this, I say, I'll continue to push and believe in Noah just as I would if he were born full-term with no complications. My response to limiting remarks: Noah has and continues to do things that the doctors said he wouldn't do, like come off the ventilator, and take a bottle. So, whose report will you believe? As for me, I believe and faith the report of the

Lord.

Tuesday, October 20, 2009, 11:14 pm, ET

Week 18, Tuesday prayer requests:

1. *Read Psalm 125 today and 126 tomorrow*
2. *Remain infection-free*
3. *Continued healing and restoration*
4. *Lower O2 support*
5. *No reflux*

Back on the bottle

Noah is doing great and had a really good day yesterday. He had an eye exam that went well; the doctor wrote: "See again in 2-3 weeks." Thank you, Jesus! Noah was given a bottle 45 minutes after his eye exam, so needless to say, that wasn't an impressive bottle; he took about 2 ml. I'm not disappointed because who would feel like eating after what they do to their eyes? They also said this happens to all babies; it's not just Noah.

I was very excited last night. The doctor isn't convinced Noah needs the surgery so they're going to see what he can do—that was music to my ears. Granted, I'm well aware he may need to have the fundo and g-tube, and if he does then we'll cross that bridge when we get to it; knowing surgery will be the last resort.

Today, Noah took 23 ml. from the bottle! He did a good job considering it was his first real time at it for about two weeks. We had speech and PT come today; I liked the PT part; I've learned some new things that I can do with Noah in encouraging his neuromuscular system. He's scheduled for a modified barium swallow on Thursday; this will tell us if he truly is aspirating (fluid going into his lungs when he swallows). Noah also had an orthopedic consult today, looking at his legs, he'll get x-rays tomorrow, and then we'll discuss what to do or how to correct the bowing (possibly splints).

The last two days have flown by, and they've both been good days—each day, Noah is getting better. I went back to see him tonight, and he had his face buried in the side of his roll; I moved the roll a bit and saw his cannula was sitting on top of his nose and he's sating 97 percent. It wasn't the nurse's fault, Noah moves his head side to side and can manipulate those prongs at times. I watched him for a good eight minutes to see how he'd do without them being in his nose, and he did well; he went to 88 percent, and his heart rate didn't drop.

I think as the night progressed, he got a little agitated and was ready to go back to bed because his sats started dropping, then his heart rate dropped. He calmed down once he got back in the bed; Mommy already left, so that mostly happened on Muh's watch.

I didn't give Noah a bath last night because I got there after the 9:00 pm feeding started, and I didn't want to wake him to bathe him. I figured he'd be okay, he won't get that dirty in one day, and I'll just bathe him tomorrow. Well, I bathed him today, and was amazed at the amount of dirt that collected in 18 hours!

We have some new moms and babies to pray for: Nicole, Sydney, Ashley, Destiny, and Mr. Brock as well; Brock isn't a NICU baby, but he has eczema and a bad food allergy. I had a chance to pray with Nicole last night. She's facing some different challenges than we did; however, it's all challenging when your baby is in the NICU.

I've started penning my thoughts about writing a book. My childhood friend called me tonight about some thoughts and ideas she's had, not knowing the conversation that I had with myself earlier in the day. Our conversation was confirmation to me to make a move, take action, and put some things together. I don't know all the how, what, or who, but I do know how to ask questions to get to the answer.
Side note. It only took me eight years to bring this book to life. The timing, is irrelevant.

Until next time. Sleep well my Prince Noah; Mommy loves you.

Wednesday, October 21, 2009, 10:17 pm, ET

Week 18, Wednesday prayer requests:

1. *Read Psalm 127*
2. *Remain infection-free*
3. *No reflux*
4. *Accelerated development*
5. *Healing of hips/no pain*
6. *Continue well with bottle*

Noah is about to hit 8 pounds!

His weight last night was 7 pounds, 15 ounces. Today was a busy day for him; I just need to do a day in the life of Noah. They were able to squeeze him in for the barium swallow late morning, which was great. That meant he didn't have to stop taking a bottle just to wait on doing the test and the results. The test came back negative for aspiration—wonderful news! It was neat to watch how they do it. The solution doesn't look good at all, but it wasn't bad enough for Noah not to take it. They mixed the barium with what he normally gets (formula and breastmilk). This means he can continue with his bottle with the mixture the way it is. Noah just needs assistance by giving lip and tongue support to keep a good suck.

Radiology came yesterday and looked at his hips. The results warranted them coming back to do an ultrasound on both of his hips; it looks like they're both dislocated. I'll get the final report tomorrow along with a treatment plan, but the x-ray techs saw it. I think one hip is in a little more than the other, but they'll both need treatment. I'm asking the same questions: "How did this happen? Is it new or something he's had? What's the treatment for it?" I've asked these questions already, but not to the right doctors yet, so I hope to have answers tomorrow.

In addition to being able to get a bottle twice a day, a technique I learned from PT yesterday is helping. If I place my hands on his shoulder, apply slight pressure, and suggest a downward motion, it helps to relax his muscles and his body. I'm working on a "good and soothing touch." Until I'm able to attempt infant mas sage, this other technique will serve both of us well.

I'm still trying to figure out the oxygen thing. We learned that the oxygen cord or knob wasn't right, which meant the oxygen wasn't working properly. When I got there today, the cannulas were hanging out of his nose, but he was having no issues even when pitching a fit. What we can't figure out is when we put the cannula back in his nose he doesn't do as well, or should I say we haven't been able to wean him down to 1/16 and keep him there. We (me, nurse, RT) considered just taking them off and seeing what Noah did, but the doctors don't take to kindly to making changes without their consent first.

Yesterday the doctor said, "We're making progress. Well, no we're not, but we're finding out what Noah needs and addressing his needs." I disagree with him—we are making progress; in finding out and addressing what Noah needs, we're getting closer to coming home. I'm feeling a little overwhelmed tonight because I'm wondering if we're ever going to go home. I was so excited about the results of the barium swallow test and then felt sucker punched about his hips. I know this is going to come to an end soon.

I was so touched last night. Some of the younger children at church often ask me about Noah, how he is, and when he's coming home. It just really touched my heart to know that even the little ones ask about Noah and pray for him.

Princess Indy very well may go home next week! I'm so

excited for them and will miss them very much. That just means we are one day closer to having our official play date!

"...When my heart is overwhelmed lead me to the rock that is higher than I..." (Psalm 61:2)

Thursday, October 22, 200,9 11:42 pm, ET

Week 18, Thursday prayer requests:

1. *Read Psalm 128 (Friday's chapter)*
2. *Remain infection-free*
3. *Continue progressing with bottle feedings*
4. *Hips to go back in socket*
5. *Accelerated development*

Bearer of bad news

Gosh, lately I feel like every time I start writing here I'm the bearer of bad news. Although I do work to highlight or point out good or positive things that have happened or been said, I feel like they're overshadowed by one more issue to deal with.

Noah is doing pretty well with his bottle; he did 18 ml. this afternoon and 22 ml. this evening. We're going on a schedule of 9:00 am and 9:00 pm for Mommy, Noah, and bottle time. The doctor is giving us this week to get it together and see just what Noah will do with the bottle. In other words, Noah has to do well and steadily make progress with the amount, or we have to go the fundo and g-tube route.

The reflux is still happening, but not as bad. Dr. P stopped by with a host of students—I'm glad they couldn't see my face because I wasn't in a mood for lots of eyes and wasn't inviting them in. Anyway, he checked Noah's hernias for swelling and said they were less swollen, and was checking the plan for surgery, and the bottle progress. I think since the reflux Noah's experiencing now isn't life threatening, we won't need the fundo—the last resort, and if we can avoid it, we should.

I still haven't talked to a pediatric orthopedist about both of his hips being dislocated, but I did talk to the neonatologist taking care of Noah. He informed me that Noah's hips have created a conundrum. The harness that they would put Noah in to fix the problem will most likely create additional and worse issues. Because of how he'd be situated in the harness, it would more than likely cause all of his hernias to get bigger, which would be bad; it would push his diaphragm up, which could impair his breathing; and make the reflux much worse. With all of that being the case, it's not worth taking those risks to repair his hips at this point. I still have to find out what that means as far as physical and occupational therapy goes.

I'm thankful for the nurses we've had on days and the past few nights. I had a mini meltdown today. It could very well be attributed to hormones, but nonetheless, I was a cry baby for a good part of the day. I so want to say, *"What else?"* but I know better, so I'm working hard to say, *"Nothing else; that's the last issue."* At times, I want to bury my head in the sand, and other times I want to reach out and touch someone, and not in a friendly way.

I recognize that I have anger issues. At both hospitals when we had the family conference, the doctors told me not to feel guilty about the events of Noah's birth and outcome; basically, "It's not my fault this happened." I didn't then, and I don't feel guilty now because I know I did everything I knew to do while I was pregnant. During that first meeting, and even now after the second, I'm still angry; in fact, I'm angrier than before. I'm angry no one listened to me; I'm angry about the lack of communication with the hospital and doctors, and I'm angry about what the nurses said to me. I have to find a healthy way to release these angry feelings and not let them invade my space. They don't consume me, yet I know they're there. I've done a lot of forgiving through this process; I'm just not there with them yet.

I could write forever, but I'm tired and have to get an early start tomorrow. Thank you, Lord, for your mercy and grace and help me to find a peace concerning this situation. Even now I hear the Lord's Prayer: "...as we forgive those that trespass against us..."

Friday, October 23, 2009, 1:09 pm, ET

Woo hoo! Noah took his 40 ml. bottle this morning like a champ! He was fussy taking it yesterday, but not today. I've learned that the reflux will hit at certain times and make it hard to take the bottle, and he likes to use the bathroom when he eats—what goes in must come out! But he did very well; I expect him to do as well if not better this evening.

Noah has surpassed the 8 pound, mark—he weighed 8 pounds, 2 ounces on Wednesday night and he's filling his clothes out quite nicely.

Saturday, October 24, 2009, 7:28 pm, ET

Week 18, Saturday prayer requests:

1. *Read Psalm 129*
2. *Remain infection-free*
3. *No reflux*
4. *Healing of hips*

Unraveling

Noah's been doing very good with his bottle; he had over 20 ml. last night and 25 ml. this morning. He had an episode on me this morning; he was finished with his bottle, and his feeding had stopped, but somewhere in there, he refluxed, and it caused him to bottom out. It wasn't as bad as they have been in the past, but it did catch me off guard because he hasn't done that in a while. By the time the nurse came into the room, I had him just about settled. Dr. P stopped by to check on Noah first thing this morning, and before the episode—he was shocked at how much milk he was taking; that was a good sign. Since this episode, I'm not sure what that might mean as far as surgery is concerned.

We're on this 9:00 am and 9:00 pm schedule now, and

I'm not quite adjusted to it yet. Getting up so early gives me an incentive to go to bed earlier, but it's still hard to do. By the time I finish laundry, get ready for the next day, get ready for bed, and unwind—it's 1:00 am. It's not helping that I wake up several times during the night as well. I've been having unsettling dreams, I won't call them nightmares, but they're still unnerving—I don't know where they're coming from. I haven't been going to sleep with the TV on, so maybe it's my subconscious thoughts that I tune out while awake. Wherever they're coming from, I'd like them to stop.

I feel like I'm unraveling or losing my grip on myself concerning the situation. I'm making the best of things, but I feel like a piece of me is dying on the inside, and then I feel bad for feeling this way. Part of my issues seem so trivial or minor (outside looking in), but rational or irrational, the small things are big things for me now. I just wish I could shut my mind off for half a day. I can say Noah brings me so much joy. Maybe this is all just hormonal psychobabble; whatever the case I'm just ready for Noah to be home, with whatever equipment and help he needs.

This too shall pass, Naomi. Just hold on and keep the faith. Someone mentioned the difference of holding versus hanging on this week, and I'm holding on.

A nurse from the other hospital made Noah a beautiful quilt. I can't wait to take it to him. Thank you!

Week 19
Set me up for success

Sunday, October 25, 2009, 8:07 am, ET

Week 19, Sunday prayer requests:

1. *Read Psalm 130*
2. *Remain infection-free*
3. *God to touch Noah's hips and put them back in place (pain-free in the meantime)*
4. *Wean from O2*
5. *Continue progress with bottle*
6. *Restful and peaceful sleep (for both of us)*
7. *Indy to go home this week and THRIVE!*

Praying for sleep

Noah had a good day yesterday. He took 35 ml. from the bottle last night and yet again surprised the doctor! The doctor wanted to wean the O2, so he did it while Noah was asleep in my arms. That lasted for about 5-8 minutes, and then he dropped out on me. His heart rate dropped pretty badly, and it scared his nurse, but once he got that little bit of flow back, he was fine. So, we're still working on that.

Thank you, Missy, for the prayer of sleep. I've not thought of doing that before for myself. I pray for restful and peaceful sleep over Noah and for Indy, but for whatever reason hadn't extended the prayer to myself, I sure will now.

I'm off to feed Noah and can't wait to report on what amazing things he's done today!

Tuesday, October 27, 2009, 12:53 am, ET

Week 19, Tuesday prayer requests:

1. *Read Psalm 131 and 132*
2. *Remain infection-free*
3. *Progress with bottle feedings*
4. *Direction/insight about surgeries needed*

Drained

Yesterday and today have been emotionally draining. Noah is doing much better than his mother. He's still sweet and displaying his wonderful disposition. He did pretty well with his bottle yesterday morning and had a pretty uneventful first half of the day.

I got to see Indy twice yesterday, and my how big she has

gotten. To my knowledge, she went home today, so I said my "see you laters" to Jamie, Jenny, and Indy last night. Saying goodbye was especially hard, Noah and Indy are nine days apart, so we've been together for four months. Even though I had a feeling they'd go home before us, it was still hard to see them go. By no means do I begrudge them and that should not even have to be said. I'm excited, so excited that they're home, in an oh so loving environment where they can grow, and Indy will thrive. Because of our walk together, I've gained great friends and have met some awesome saints and prayer warriors through our connection. So, GO INDY GO! Noah and I will see you soon!

I'm still on the 9:00 am and 9:00 pm feeding schedule. After visiting the Schaffers, I went to feed Noah. I've really come to learn his body language and detect when something isn't right with him. As he was eating, he just didn't seem like himself. He was more fussy and agitated, and I had to burp him way sooner and more often than usual. So much so, that after only taking 15 ml., I stopped and just asked the nurse to do the rest via the tube. He was doing this gagging thing, but nothing was coming up until finally, it started coming up and he couldn't get it out. Usually, when this happens, Noah will either spit it up or swallow it, but neither was happening. It caught my attention because he just couldn't catch his breath and whatever was not coming up or going down. I called the nurse and told her he needed to be suctioned. As she's trying to figure out how to get the suction to work right, Noah isn't moving, turning colors and his heart rate and O2 were way low.

Thankfully, I've seen it enough and know to turn up his O2. After three and a half nurses (some came to help, and some came to watch), they finally got the suction working and had to bag him to get him level again. Did I mention the feeding was still going? It got stopped after they bagged him.

The cause of the initial problem was that the feeding tube was in the wrong place; it wasn't in far enough. The kicker for me was that two different nurses couldn't read the numbers on the tube, so I'm not sure how long the tube was in the wrong place. I can say listening for the "whoosh" of air is not the best method to determine if a feeding tube is in the right spot. So, needless to say, I was pissed. After being scared, I was just outright mad, because yet again we have equipment that either wasn't working properly or wasn't being used correctly. I asked the charge nurse to go through and check every piece of equipment that would be used on Noah to make sure they were working properly before I left. We've come too far for something that could be avoided to happen because of faulty equipment and dare I say, inexperienced staff.

This isn't the first time we've had equipment issues, and we've only been here two and a half weeks. Noah is often assigned newer nurses because he's an older baby and not as "critical" as the newer and younger babies. Thankfully, he doesn't require the amount of attention he once did, but whoever his caretaker is needs to be made fully aware of what can happen. I'm to the point now (and have been, just ready to be more vocal), to just teach me how to use this equipment: the suction, the bag, the feeding pump, the feeding tube, etc. I'm there enough where I've watched and learned some things, but I want and need to know the proper way. If you can teach students, then teach me. The more I know how to do; I will feel comfortable doing, especially when we get home.

Have I mentioned lately that I'm ready to go home? I'm ready to go home.

The doctor suggested getting a portable DVD player so Noah could get additional stimulation from movies: sound, colors, and movement. Since he's staying up 3-4 hours at a time, I went and got him one. It was funny to watch Noah respond to the sounds. We played music while he ate and then watched a movie afterward; his facial expressions were priceless!

I talked to one of the orthopedic doctors and three students/residents this afternoon. This doctor hasn't evaluated Noah, but his counterpart has. I'm not sure why he came by—He's the sixth ortho doctor that's come to see him. After I had asked the doctor some questions, he looked at Noah's x-rays and said he thinks Noah dislocated his hips in utero. I didn't get into how that happened because he went on to talk about treatment. Like I mentioned before, at this point they aren't going to do any treatment. They want to fix the current problems and then address the hips as an outpatient.

As of today, we're going forward with the fundo, g-tube, and hernia surgeries. We're waiting for a date from the surgeon—we should know something tomorrow. The doctor and I have agreed about the surgery, but for two different reasons. God can still intervene.

I went to see Dr. S today; I wanted to thank him for some things and pick his brain about some other things.

Your words of encouragement, your advice as different situations arise, and your prayers mean a lot, Thanks!

Someone said it must be hard for me to go back to our old hospital. As crazy as it sounds, I'm comfortable there; it's home for me in a sense. I spent four months there, and that's what I know; it's familiar and comfortable, and dare I say, safe. I get a feeling of safety because I know the people there. As much as I hate to, I can cry among them and feel like it's okay because they know my journey.

Let me end this entry with positive notes. I'm thankful we had a nurse we were familiar with today. I asked if we could have her knowing the chances were very slim, and we got her! I was praying the whole way to the hospital for God to work on me (my attitude) and whichever nurse we would have for the day. Having her gave me such a feeling of peace and put a huge smile on my face this morning.
Muh is on bath duty now, this gives her and Noah some bonding time and is a source of laughs for me—the two of them are comical together. Lastly, Noah took 47 ml. from his bottle tonight! I believe that before he has surgery, he'll get to take a full 60 ml. bottle.
A quote from Ram Dass that has stuck with me, "Everything in your life is there as a vehicle for your transfor-

mation. Use it!"

Tuesday, October 27, 2009, 5:44 pm, ET

Week 19, Tuesday prayer requests:

1. *Read Psalm 132*
2. *Remain infection-free*
3. *Accelerated development*

Surgery is scheduled

Noah had a good day today. He's such a wonderful little boy and handles things so well. The nasal cannula stopped working, it wasn't getting the flow, and thankfully the nurse caught it. I'm having to start asking more questions of the RTs here. I'm used to seeing the RTs and know the routine from across the street, but things work differently here.

We have a surgery date of next Tuesday, November 3. We're scheduled for a fundo also, called a Nissen wrap, a g-tube, and umbilical hernia repair. They won't do the groin hernias just yet; the doctors said it would be too much for Noah. Depending on how long we're in the hospital post-op will determine if the hernias get fixed before we leave or if we get it done as an outpatient. We could very well be home before Thanksgiving! Oh, what a gift that would be!!

I met with the Family Services Coordinator which was very helpful. The information alone was helpful, but there are things I can learn from her. She has a child who had encountered some of the same things Noah did in utero. She's a wealth of information because of her job, and she's already walked (and still is) the path that I'm about to embark on.

Wednesday, October 28, 2009, 9:27 am, ET

Week 19, Wednesday prayer requests:

1. *Read Psalm 133*
2. *Remain infection-free*
3. *Accelerate development*
4. *Progress with bottle*

GO, NOAH, GO!

I am so excited! Noah took his first full bottle last night! That's right; he took a full 60 ml. at dinner time last night. Thank you, to a couple of our day nurses, for encouraging me to use the other nipple, and for having that conversation and relaying information to each other. When I fed Noah at noon yesterday, we started with the slow flow preemie nipple and then changed to the blue nipple half way through the feeding time. We were thinking that by changing nipples, he wouldn't have to work so hard and not get tired as quickly. Changing the two nipples didn't seem to make that much difference during the day, so his nurse wanted to start him out with the regular yellow nipple last night. I was a little hesitant because we had tried that last week and the flow was just too fast—I didn't want to give them "another reason" to say why Noah couldn't do something. She got a chair and sat in there with me as I fed him and he did it like a champ! He paced himself so well; it took 30 minutes, many burps included, so we were all good! Thank you Lord! Thank you, for helping Noah and giving him the strength. He continues to get better and stronger every day.

Noah and I finished the Veggie Tales movie that he and Muh started. It was a good movie composed of several short stories, and all talking about how it's okay to be different and big things come in small packages. There was a scripture from Psalm 139 that rang out from the movie last night; "He knows all about us, He formed us and find comfort knowing that we were fearfully and wonderfully made."

Thank you, my awesome prayer warriors for your unfailing love and faithful prayers. The journey has been long, but I feel comforted that I don't travel it alone. When I'm overcome with emotions or having trouble seeing the light, I read the heartfelt comments and prayers for Noah as well as myself on the website. Helping me look beyond here and now, and looking 1, 5, 18, and 25 years down the road and picturing the handsome, smart, athletic, well-rounded and exceptional son and young man that Noah has become.

Thank you, Muh, for being my rock. For teaching me what it means to be an intercessor and a worshiper. I find myself singing to Noah in the mornings when I go in and wake him up. What a wonderful way to wake up. I never thought I'd do this, let alone like it. Thank you, for your steadfast faithfulness and endless prayers that you bathe Noah in (your seed and your seed's seed is blessed). Thanks to Pap, for sharing Muh, and loving on Noah. As scary as it may sometimes be, you handle it all in stride. Pop Pop, you rock—We're waiting for the next installment of the Tiger Woods book.

Some of the nurses have gotten sucked into Noah's World. One of the nurses we had last week came by to check in on us—this was so sweet. She was telling me that Noah is all hers when I'm not there and that they have some of the other nurses to come by and see him. Just wait until this weekend when he has on his Halloween costume from one of his former nurses!

Create a **great** day!

Friday, October 30, 2009, 3:14 pm, ET

Week 19, Friday prayer requests:

1. *Read Psalm 135*
2. *Remain infection-free*
3. *Accelerated development*
4. *Reflux and umbilical hernia surgery on Tuesday*

There's more than one "preemie channel"

He's doing great and really enjoying his bottles, taking a full one this morning, 45 ml. last night, and a full bottle yesterday afternoon. The day before the bottle didn't go so well, but that was because we changed nipples on him again.

We've had the same nurse for the last three days which is very nice. She taught me how to put the NG feeding tube down (that was so not fun), but I'm glad I had the chance to learn how to do it. She also taught me how to push Noah's current medicines, how to check them for the right dosage, and attach it to the tube port and stuff, so that was really nice. It's not necessarily nice to push them but to be more active in his care, especially since I'll have to do it when he comes home.

Surgery is still on for next Tuesday morning. I got an unofficial second opinion today and the conclusion was the same, surgery is the best and safest way to bring Noah home. This is good because Noah will very likely be able to come home a week or so after the surgery. It could also help him to reduce the amount of O2 support.

I met with the speech therapist yesterday and got clarity on the nipple and feeding issue. We had a nice chat and got on the same page. Our ultimate goal is for Noah to be successful eating in the safest manner. Right now, this means using the slow flow nipple and eating by bottle twice a day. I'm glad we had the conversation even though we'll be at a different point next week after surgery.

I'm learning (accepting) that there are several substations in the preemie channel—it's a station that I don't like and one I don't want to watch, but am being forced to.

Lord, help me walk this out and learn not to my own under

standing. You are faithful, and Your will will be done.

Saturday, October 31, 2009, 7:00 pm, ET

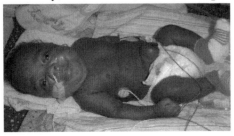

Week 19, Saturday prayer requests:

1. *Read Psalm 136*
2. *Remain infection-free*
3. *Progress with bottle*
4. *Accelerated development*

Toe-jam

Noah is doing great! We've increased our bottle feeds to three times a day—YAY! Prayerfully, with this progress and momentum, we'll be able to bottle feed first thing after the surgery. Noah now has a swing in his room to go along with the bouncy seat, mobile, sound machine, and DVD player. What else could a little boy ask for? He, of course, hasn't actually asked for any of it, but I think I've hit my limit as to what I can bring in. It will be funny to watch me take it all home when it's time to leave.

There isn't much to update on today, he's doing well in

all areas, and we're just waiting for the surgery. The doctor said they'd most likely put Noah on the vent Monday afternoon and give him the paralytic. They'll probably do this until the surgery on Tuesday. They do it this way so as much air can get out of his abdomen as possible, giving the surgeon as much room as can possible to work with.

We had a new nurse today who has taken some getting used to. She had her own agenda which just messed our feeding routine up completely. I've learned to be more vocal with this these past few days than the whole time we've been at this. I know, how in the world could I become more vocal? I really don't say a whole lot as far as how Noah is cared for unless it's just way out of line. But what I've learned is as he and I are getting the routine down with chow time, that's something we don't need to keep experimenting with.

Can anyone explain to me how a size 3 diaper is floating around the NICU and ends up on my kid? Granted, it was on nice and snug, and it did its job of containing the poo, but come on, a size 3? The nurse told me she was in a fix and was scrambling for a diaper and that's what she was able to find; I'm still baffled.

Did you know that toe-jam is not a respecter of age or size? I am in awe every time I clean between Noah's toes and find toe-jam in there, regardless if he's had socks on or not. That's just too funny to me. It's amazing to me all the wonderful things I'm learning in the world of motherhood.

Week 20
I can see his face!

Monday, November 2, 2009, 9:50 pm, ET

Week 20, Monday prayer requests:

1. *Read Psalm 138 and 139 (tomorrow)*
2. *Successful surgery*
3. *Remain infection-free*
4. *Accelerated development*
5. *Mommy to de-stress*

(Breast)milk does a body good

Noah has weighed in at 9 pounds! Who knew breast-milk packed so many calories? We had a wonderful visit this evening and a good day yesterday. Yesterday morning was the first time I fed Noah all by myself. Normally, if something weird happens it's with the nurses, and it's the bed that ends up getting fed. After Noah had taken his whole bottle, I went to get his last burp out and realized he was wet and slimy. I didn't recall seeing or hearing him throw up, but I realized I was soaking wet. There was milk all over me! The clamp to the end of the feeding tube wasn't on tight so even though Noah strained to take the bottle—he'd do it whatever, whichever way to make it happen; he pushed the fluid back up the tube and right out all over me. I was late for church that day.

My church family gave Noah and me a welcome home shower, and it was just beautiful. They showered us with beautiful gifts and a lot of love. Indy's mom, Jenny, made it out and it was wonderful to see her. I miss Jenny, but I'm glad she's home with Indy and doing well. The message at church that day dealt with the mighty men of God waking up (Joel and 2 Samuel). The thing that stuck with me was, "Let things be birthed from your experience." Let your experience work for you, and each day I'm seeing how this experience can "work" for me.

Tonight I got to give Noah his bath. Giving him a bath was nice, even though it was supposed to be Muh's time. Noah was very patient and peaceful while giving him his bath. I took my time, and he didn't fuss, even through washing and brushing his hair. We had talked all day about the procedure tomorrow and what they were going to do to him tonight (start an IV, put him on the ventilator, and paralyze him). I trust you, Lord, and Noah is entrusted to you. I know you know the plans you have for him.

We liked the nurse today; she was very helpful. We had a good visit with PT again; we talked about things to do to help and kind of work around the hip dislocation issue. We switched over doctors, so we're working with a whole new crew, UGH!

Do you understand the words coming out of my mouth?

I'm beginning to think I need to learn another language, French, Spanish, sign language, or something besides plain English because that's not working. I'm livid, though not as bad as earlier. They started Noah on a new medicine Friday. The doctor at the time and I talked about this medicine and discussed its pros and cons several days ago. The conversation was based around Noah being able to safely take his bottle and the impact it would have on his development. We discussed the importance and pleasure Noah expressed being able to take his bottle and the bonding it offered us. The doctor shared that this particular medicine would cause Noah's muscles to relax too much, so he wouldn't be able to control the milk and he'd lose the ability to eat by mouth. Based on what we were looking at, and what we want, we decided to hold off on the medicine.

As I fed Noah yesterday, I heard bits and pieces during rounds, and they mentioned this medicine. I figured they weren't talking about Noah because he wasn't on that med, so I paid it no mind. The nurse today was asking me about the meds given to Noah and if I knew what they were and what they're for and I said yes. She just looked at me strangely, so I started naming what he gets, and then she adds this other drug.

Naomi was not happy, at all. I'm pissed off because in

three days, I've had at least five different nurses (that's not the problem) and I've asked them, "What's different or changed with his treatment? What's been added? What was discussed in rounds?" I should cover the bases with these questions and be in the know. Not one of them noticed or took the time to notice that a new medicine was added. What else can I ask to gather information? I'm at the hospital at least twice a day, every day, and usually for several hours; I'm a hands-on mom. I ask questions because I want to know how to take care of my son, not just at home or when it's time to go home but while he's in the hospital too. Noah and I are the constant in this equation—they are the variables, and I do not understand the communication difficulties. This is becoming a major pain in my you know what. The itch in me has been aroused and starting to surface. I'm not rude or obnoxious, but I'm not being Pollyanna either.

Starting a new med seems simple. However, being told that everything is the same and that nothing is different, is not okay with me. If Noah did start having negative effects from the meds, I'd think it was because of one thing when in actuality it could be from the new medication. Today's issue is the straw that broke the camel's back. I was so bent I had to, *had* to leave the hospital to get some fresh air before I spoke or did anything else.

What added more fuel to the fire today is recalling the day he went to three bottle feeds a day. I arrived back at the hospital a few minutes before it was time to start, and the tube feeding was already going. Had I not said anything, the nurse wouldn't have checked to see the new orders. And people wonder why I want my medical records and why I don't want to leave the hospital. I've gotten much better at leaving because I'm no good exhausted; however, just how comfortable can I feel when I'm getting no information or the wrong information?

My goal is simple: to help them help me, help Noah, and get us home in the safest most efficient manner.

Tuesday, November 3, 2009, 9:12 pm, ET

Week 20, Tuesday prayer requests:

1. *Read Psalm 139 and 140 (tomorrow)*
2. *We're home before we get to Psalm 150!*
3. *Remain infection-free*
4. *Quick and whole recovery*
5. *Accelerated development*
6. *Off the vent tonight and able to eat tomorrow*

Surgery went well!

Noah is doing great. The surgery went well with no complications except for having to put in another IV. He's resting well and likely to come off the vent tonight. The surgeon believes Noah's groin was mainly full of fluid, and not hernias—this is good news. I'm thankful we can see his penis again. The swelling had gotten to the point many of the nurses didn't realize he'd been circumcised. The swelling made things bad, but Dr. P worked that out too (literally). Tomorrow we should have a discussion, along with a plan started as far as next steps and discharge time frame.

Thank you to those who came to sit with me during the surgery and all of you wonderful saints for lifting Noah and myself in prayer this morning. Although I was a little unnerved in the beginning, my inner man did get calm and peaceful.

God is so faithful, patient, and kind. A friend gave and I've tucked the thought, "How would Jesus react?" back to the front of my mind. I try to filter my thoughts before they reach my tongue, so this reminds me of a different approach. I had the opportunity to talk to the chief neonatologist for quite a while this afternoon, and it was a very productive conversation. I can't describe how good it was to be able to feel comfortable to not only express my concerns and grievances but to know they're being heard and will be addressed. The conversation shifted several times, but it was all relevant and beneficial.

I then spoke with the nurse manager at length upon her request—I was going to put it off until tomorrow. We talked about the equipment and communication issues. I was so happy to hear her response, and together we'll be able to turn these experiences into teachable moments, and most of all strengthen the partnership of the nursing staff with the parent(s)—including me. The music to my ears from all of this is that we may have a core group of nurses that work with us until we go home, I am so excited!

I've learned to work with the system, regardless of my feelings or desires. I'm reminded of the scripture, *"In all thy ways acknowledge Him and He shall give you the desires of your heart." (Psalm 37)*

I went to a class presented by a local pediatrician about common illnesses seen during the first year of life. Before starting, there was an expectant mom who was voicing her desires to not be pregnant anymore and ready for the baby to come now if she wanted to (five weeks early). I know she didn't really mean it, I kindly mentioned to her she might what to reconsider what she asks for. I just said, "As miserable as you may be, you really don't want to spend time in the NICU. Encourage her to stay in until you're closer to your due date."

Did I cross the line in saying this to her? I don't know. Now, I think I may have, but at the time I definitely didn't think so. I'm not trying to get in her business, but she put it out there, and I really don't think we (people) think about the ramifications of what we say. I'm not saying her words would cause early labor, but I just want to remind people to think before speaking. I'm totally over analyzing the situation but what I wouldn't give to have been able to carry Noah to five weeks before or to even his due date; I would have taken another day.

Mommy is way tired and going to sleep. Before I do, I want to share some scriptures from the past few days that spoke to me.

"I will praise you, O Lord, with all my heart; before the 'gods' I will sing your praise. Though I walk in the midst of trouble, you preserve my life; you stretch out your hand against the anger of my foes, with your right hand you save me. The Lord

will fulfill his purpose for me; your love, O Lord, endures forever- do not abandon the works for your hands." (Psalm 138:1, 7, 8)

"O Lord, you have searched me and you know me. You know when I sit and when I rise; you perceive my thoughts from afar. You discern my going out and my lying down; you are familiar with all my ways. Before a word is on my tongue you know it completely, O Lord. You hem me in- behind and before; you have laid your hand upon me. Such knowledge is too wonderful for me, too lofty for me to attain. For you created my inmost being; you knit me together in my mother's womb. I praise you because I am fearfully and wonderfully made; your works are wonderful, I know that full well. Search me, O God, and know my heart; test me and know my anxious thoughts. See if there is any offensive way in me, and lead me in the way everlasting." (Psalm 139:1-6, 13, 14, 23 and 24)

-Amen

Wednesday, November 4, 2009, 10:55 pm, ET

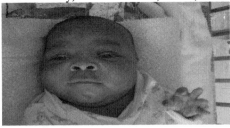

Week 20, Wednesday prayer requests:

1. *Read Psalm 141*
2. *Remain infection-free*

3. *Accelerated development*
4. *Keep heart rate up*

Maybe, hopefully, going home next week

Noah is off the nasal cannula and breathing room air! He came off the cannula sometime this morning; after the shift change and before 9:00 am; thanks, Dr. P! I cried when I saw him; this is the first time I've seen his whole face with nothing on it. Thank you Lord; it's the little (they're really not little) things that make a difference.

Noah is breathing on his own, and he took a bottle twice today. He got started with 15 ml. of straight breastmilk and will increase gradually. No more mixing with formula! I learned how to use the g-tube via nurse demonstration, so I'll probably feed him once myself that way—it seems fairly simple.

I wish I still had milk so I could put him to breast, but I still have freezers full—thanks, friends for letting me keep my milk at your house! The plan was to do just breastmilk, but we'll add a couple of formula bottles in there a day.

I've been on cloud nine all day, it was wonderful. Even though Noah's heart rate started dropping, I was still able to enjoy the day. When his heart rate dropped, his O2 levels stayed in the 90s. They started one of the meds back, and I think that will make a difference for him. That reminds me, Noah is down to just two medicines a day and iron!

We selected a pediatrician, so that's one less thing we have to do. We're also looking at going home the beginning of next week! Looking forward to tomorrow's report!

Week 21
Dr. God, the ultimate physician

Sunday, November 8, 2009, 5:53 pm, ET

Week 21, Sunday prayer requests:

1. *Read Psalm 144*
2. *Remain infection-free*
3. *All issues cleared before coming home*

Our going home day is coming!

Noah is doing well. He's recovering from surgery and making great progress! His milk intake as of this afternoon is now 70 ml. and he took every bit of it. In working to get everything ready for him to come home and to get him to take his bottle with other people, I let the nurses give him a bottle once a day. Today was the first day he took all of his bottles from a nurse. Normally, he only takes 20 ml. before he quits and they put the rest down the g-tube. All mommy can do is laugh because he takes it all for me with no problem or hesitation. He's getting his strong suck back, he'd gum the nipple and needed quite a bit of cheek support the first couple of days post-surgery, but he had a superb suck today! Go, Noah go!

Muh was worried about Noah not being able to burp, or rather not fitting in because he might not be able to do the infamous Potter belch—a well-known burp inherited from my maternal grandmother's side. Not all of the Potter descendants have this ability, and to my knowledge, it's a gift only for an elite selection of women; I've not heard the boys do it. With having the fundo and g-tube, Muh thought Noah wouldn't be able to do it. On the contrary; he has two ways of doing it now. He can and does still burp, but he also burps from the g-tube which is so funny to hear. All I can say is, good job! There's more room out than in! His burps can be so loud, and today, one of them caught his nurse off guard. And she wondered why I burped him both ways; now she understands.

Noah's bottom is better. We still do the thick, pasty stuff as a barrier, but there are no red or open sores anymore. Thank you, Jesus! Hopefully, you won't hear any more butt stories; we've moved on to the penis. I'll keep those talks and details limited; some nurses still can't tell he's been circumcised (so you see my problem).

Wednesday, Thursday, and Friday were the best days we've had in a long time. I couldn't stop smiling and was still floating on air. I'm so excited to be coming home soon and excited to see Noah's face—his whole face, every morning. They told me to bring the car seat in, and they'd start working on that test. Noah has to sit in the seat for at least 30 minutes and have no drops in his heart rate or O2. I was so excited, "I get to bring the car seat! I get to bring the car seat! Oh crap; I've got to go get a car seat!" So I went to get one, and watching me install it in the car was such a sight. It would have been so much easier if my car was newer and had the latches in the back seat, but I got it in, it works, and it's safe!

I'm getting there, and our day is fast approaching; **we're going home!** I think of all of the babies we've seen come and go and cheered them on along the way, especially when it was their turn to go home. And here we are, our day is actually approaching, Thank you, God! We're headed into week 21, yet there's light; I can see the light, and I welcome it.

I read a quote the other day from Peace Pilgrim, "If you realized how powerful your thoughts are, you would never think a negative thought." As I work through some of my thoughts and fears, I'm reminded that I can do all things through Christ who strengthens me. I have to trust that God does know what He's doing (sounds silly I know) more so I have to trust myself that God trusts me, and know that things will work out when we get home.

Until later...

Monday, November 9, 2009, 6:13 pm, ET

Week 21, Monday prayer requests:

1. *Read Psalm 145*
2. *Remain infection-free*
3. *Resolve heart rate issues*
4. *Complete wholeness*
5. *Baby Phil and family*

Our homecoming is on hold

Now we're looking at coming home next week. We have to go five days without a medical intervention before the hospital will discharge us. We had a minor incident that required O2 (this hasn't happened since before surgery). When Noah's heart rate dropped previously, he only needed a little stimulation. We also have a consult with neurology. Dr. P thinks Noah had what looked like a seizure on Saturday. They checked one of the medicine levels and adjusted it, and based on the neuro consult they want to do another EEG this week. An ortho doctor came by today as well; they said there's nothing they can do for Noah's hips at this point or any time in the near future. The earliest they could do anything would be when he is five years old, provided he's walking.

On a brighter note, we've increased Noah's feedings to 75 ml., and he gets a bottle four times a day now. I'm still confused on how I can give that much milk in a tube in less than five minutes, but when it was NG feedings, it had to go in over an hour. I'll ask this question later today. Overall, we're doing well and are in a good place. We're expecting and planning to be home before Thanksgiving.

Monday, November 9, 2009, 11:19 pm, ET

These messengers keep getting in my way

I'm not going to say I can't cope, but I feel as if I'm losing my grip on things. I'm disgusted with talking in circles with the staff. Dr. B always tells me, "Don't shoot the messenger," whenever he's about to give me news. Well, some of the messengers keep getting in the way and they're catching my frustration. I understand how the system is setup to work (part of it anyway), but I find it illogical to keep doing the same thing and expect a different result. Why talk to, or send my questions to several different people, none of which can answer my question, only to get several different answers?

Don't presume you know my questions. If I say I have questions, there are things I either don't understand or need more clarity on before discharge. I don't have to see you face-to-face; I'm perfectly fine discussing things over the phone and would think that would fit your schedule just fine. I'm accommodating and flexible, yet I've reached my limit with the bureaucratic bullshit.

If you're reading this and don't understand what I'm feeling, in a way I'm glad you don't and pray that you never do.

On the bright side, we liked our nurse, tonight. She puts me in the mind of our former chatty night nurse with all her cleaning ways. She seems really sweet too. I saw Jenny and Indy today, and that was a treat. Indy has gotten so big; she looks wonderful, and Jenny is as happy as can be. Thank you, Dr. P for working hard to resolve this last issue and get us home.

Tomorrow morning, we have an eye exam.

Tuesday, November 10, 2009, 12:55 pm, ET

Week 21, Tuesday prayer requests:

1. *Read Psalm 146*
2. *Remain infection-free*
3. *Accelerated development/continued good growth*
4. *Complete wholeness*
5. *Good communication between mom and staff*

Is this depression?

Noah is doing great! He had a good night last night and is having a good day today. His heart rate dropped once and came right back up. The nurse didn't want to count it because it was so quick. I'm wondering if this counts as an "incident" since we're monitoring heart rate drops. The alarm didn't sound, the nurse just saw it. She attributed the drop to straining while using the bathroom. I think everyone's heart has stopped a time or two while going number two. Gross, but true. I do still have my sense of humor.

Thank you, Jesus! We don't see the eye people again for six months! The doctor came this morning and gave Noah a good report on his eyes—great news! I also spoke with the doctors from ortho and neuro. It found it funny that when I walked in today, the first thing the resident did was get my phone number and tell me that someone from ortho would be calling me today. When Dr. P saw me, she had the same sentiments, "Since the go between isn't working, someone from the other departments will call you today." And they did. In talking with the neuro attending, I got to see Noah's CT results.

The time with the neurologist was both disheartening and encouraging. The plan, for now, is to have another EEG tomorrow, get results before the weekend, do the car seat test over the weekend, and look at discharging the beginning of next week. Plans are always subject to change, but that's where we are today.

In reading yesterday's and today's Psalm, I was convicted for not reading it yesterday and then relieved and encouraged by what the passages said. Psalm 145:1-7, 13, 16-18 was so applicable for where I was yesterday (a reminder of who and what God is to me and what His Word says He is and what He'll do). That through this season of life, God is still God. And as time goes on I can remind myself, Noah, and others the wonderful works God has done. It just encouraged me again to remember there's purpose in all of this.

Psalm 146 is a reminder of who God is. He's an awesome, wonderful, all knowing, all powerful, all present God. He's the ultimate physician, and He has the final say. Verse 6 says, "The Maker of heaven and earth, the sea, and everything in them—the Lord, who remains faithful forever."

Verse 1-2 says, "Praise the Lord. Praise the Lord, O my soul. I will praise the Lord all my life; I will sing praise to my God as long as I live." My spirit jumped when I read that this morning to Noah. In essence, don't lose your song. Through everything, keep your praise. I've not lost my praise, thank God. I was at a place last night where it didn't seem to matter if I had a song left or not. When my flame becomes a flicker, it's a reminder to feel encouraged and to fan that flicker until it flames again, brighter and bolder than before.

Could some of what I'm feeling be depression or post-partum depression? It could be. On some days, it's what I consider a man's worst nightmare, PMS times 100. Have I considered taking something for it? Yes. In looking at the side effects from some of the medication, it could make things worse—which I definitely don't need. Hopefully, through journaling, exercising again, and eating healthier, that will help my emotions stay consistent.

Your prayers are always appreciated. Grandpa Bill, thank you, for suggesting the flow sheet—this could benefit all of us. I've started writing my questions down and have seen the difference it makes especially with getting the nurses to help me navigate my concerns.

Blessings...

Friday, November 13, 2009, 3:24 pm, ET

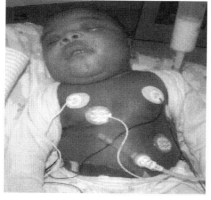

This picture was of Noah eating last night. He has two sets of leads on (one set for the hospital and one that goes to the home monitor). You can see his g-tube and the syringe in the back with the milk. He looks like he's living the high life! He was sleeping quite hard at this point.

Week 21, Friday prayer requests:

1. *Read Psalm 149*
2. *Remain infection-free*
3. *Continue good growth*
4. *Event-free weekend*

We're going home! For real this time.

YES! We are scheduled to go home on Monday! Noah is 9 pounds, 5 ounces as of last night and filling out his clothes quite nicely. He's had a busy schedule the last couple of days. He had another EEG, and the doctor says to keep him on anti-seizure medicine. He finished the hearing test they started and couldn't finish last week. Physical therapy made splints for his ankles and feet; they are so small and cute! Cary Sue wanted to be proactive in aligning his tibia and fibula, and reinforce good posture in an attempt to make standing and walking better.

We did the home monitor class yesterday, and boy, that thing is loud. It could honestly wake the dead, and that's kind of what it's supposed to do. The monitor will track his heart rate and respiration while he's sleeping.

Muh is back and gave him a bath yesterday. Noah has his grandmother wrapped around his little finger, so who knows what will happen once he's home.

We've been having bottle and bathroom issues. It's been a couple of days since Noah has taken a full bottle, which isn't normal for him. He has more gas and is more irritable while taking his bottle; I think the big part is him having a harder time going to the bathroom. It also doesn't work well in trying to suck in and push out at the same time. Whatever he doesn't take by mouth I have to put down the tube. The g-tube feedings work by gravity. I work to pace the feeding in just as if he were taking a bottle over 20 minutes. We do really well until we get close to the end and he starts pushing (as if to pass gas or make a number two). Well, when he pushes, the milk comes back up the tube. So I can have 5-10 ml. left to go, and if I don't catch it in time, Noah can push back 10-20 ml. Yesterday it took three of us to get the rest of the milk down the g-tube. One was holding the pacifier, one was stroking his head and distracting him, and I was pushing the milk in.

I did pretty well with handling everything by myself today, and we won't need a home health nurse when we go home; when I asked the nurse yesterday, she told me Noah doesn't qualify, which was music to my ears. A few weeks ago they were confident he'd be coming home with more equipment and that his care would be more complex than what it is.

He has started moving his lower legs a bit! He's never really kicked them, yet he was briefly moving them independently yesterday.

We're at the final stage of this hurry up and wait chapter of our journey. We're winding up the book of Psalm tomorrow and we'll move to Proverbs Chapter 1 starting on Sunday.

The other week when we thought Noah was coming home, I contacted the high-risk doctor that delivered him and asked her to prescribe me an antidepressant. I was becoming anxious and feeling a bit stressed about bringing Noah home and being solely responsible for his care. On top of that, I never really processed the many events that transpired over the last five months leaving my emotions all over the place. I wanted to be proactive and have antidepressant medication in case I needed to start them instead of waiting until we got home, when getting out of the house would be more challenging.

Week 22
Getting along with my new roommate

Tuesday, November 17, 2009, 5:32 pm, ET

Week 22, Tuesday prayer requests:

1. *Just pray*

Noah is home!

This will be short because I'm trying to console him, but will come back with details when I have had some time and at least an hour of sleep in my system.

The past 48 hours have been wonderful and hellacious. I got more sleep when I first went off to college. We had a trial run and roomed-in Sunday night at the hospital to make sure I was ready to take Noah home. During our room-in, I was responsible for all of his care and the nurses would only come and help if there was an emergency. I've found another person who can sleep through the monitor; I won't mention names; ahem, Grandmother. Noah was up almost all night. He finally gave up around 2:00 am, but his monitor had a mind of its own and went off every two minutes with false alarms. I can't find a word that describes worse than exhausted—this is how I feel. We have our first pediatrician appointment at 8:00 am tomorrow (whoever chose that hellish hour of the morning for an appointment has no clue), so prayerfully I get a little more sleep tonight, so I can function in the morning.

Sweet angel Noah doesn't like to be put down awake or asleep; I'm not sure where he gets this from. Even his swing and bouncy seat don't satisfy him now, so we're learning how to live together and hopefully get into the swing of things soon.

Thank you, for your continued prayers and support. If I'm not back tonight, I will return tomorrow so I can unload my thoughts and Noah's continued journey: Life outside of the NICU!

Robin and Jenny, I'm looking forward to our playdates. Once I get a week or two of being home under my belt, playtime is on!

Thursday, November 19, 2009, 4:49 pm, ET

Can you please cheer with me?

I might be able to start journaling every day or every
other day again. The past few days have been extremely
stressful; and not due to Noah, thank you, Lord!

Noah is doing really well. He went to bed at a decent
hour last night; a little after midnight. Each day is getting better with his sleep patterns. I think the more he
adjusts to the home environment, the more relaxed he's
becoming. I got him a baby Boppy pillow (thanks for the
tip, Tiffany) which is absolutely wonderful. He'll happily
sit in it for a long time; he even likes to nap in it. Dare
I say the first few nights he slept on it in the bed with
me, and on his back of course. He will lie in his bassinet, but hasn't slept a whole night in it yet; partly due
to the monitor issues. Speaking of monitors, after going
through four monitors and filling up three of them in
less than a week, we have a completely different monitor. This one is similar to the one at the hospital which
monitors his O2 saturation and his heart rate.

I got my first night of sleep—well, 90 uninterrupted
minutes if that counts. I don't mind getting up with
Noah, having known this would be par for the course of
motherhood. The challenging and frustrating part was
the doggone alarm going off continuously for no reason.
I tried all the tricks and suggestions minus adding water,
and nothing worked. It had the monitor people baffled
too. Getting the new monitor wasn't easy. You know, if it

235

wasn't for God on my side where and how would I be? They told me that Noah couldn't get this current monitor unless he was on oxygen (and that wasn't going to happen). Thankfully, the nurse practitioner was able to square that problem away for me!

Back to Noah, he is as sweet as can be. Pop Pop got to hold him for the first time on Monday. He was a little apprehensive because of the "wires" (the leads for the monitor), but he conquered that fear and got to love on his grandson! Aunt Cookie drove us home from the hospital and got to change Noah's stinky diapers. He loves on his momma and gives me kisses. He's in Muh's arms every chance he or she gets!

I'm so glad my little one is home. We took our first ride in the stroller today, Noah was awake all the way up to snapping the car seat into the stroller and fell asleep as I wheeled him up the street. I even crumbled some leaves near his ear to see how he would react; it was the same as with the monitor, no movement! Tomorrow is another day, so we'll see what happens. As we were on our walk, I checked the monitor to make sure everything was working right, and it was. As we started walking again, I heard the "Beep, beep. Beep, beep" of the monitor. I was a little panicked because I had just checked the machine and Noah was fine. I looked at the machine, and the numbers were good, Noah looked good, so where is the beeping coming from? Ha, ha it was one of the cable company trucks backing up! I felt so silly, but that's the reality I'm in right now, and I'm institutionally conditioned by that beeping sound. In reading one of mom's journal, she alluded to having PTSD when it came to the alarms (and I understand that). You understand it, or it makes more sense if you've been through it (with a child or adult).

We're still working the bottle thing out. The first day or two, Noah took his whole bottle when he got it; the first time in a long time. Now, we're back to taking anywhere from 30-50 ml. Muh and I both think in part it's because he's not hungry. I hate force-feeding him through the tube and want to give him the opportunity to get hungry. I just don't want him to become dependent on the tube and forget how to suck and swallow. That's definitely a question for the pediatrician tomorrow.

There is so much more to say, but it's chow time for the lil' guy, so until next time.

Weeks 23 & Beyond
The first year out of the NICU

Surviving the NICU was a major accomplishment and huge emotional task. Life outside of it was just as challenging if not more because my support system changed—I was no longer a visitor yet the caregiver and learning to navigate systems was nerve-wracking and emotionally draining.

Noah came home a week before Thanksgiving. This is my favorite holiday, and I have such wonderful child-hood memories as this was the one time of year all of my family and extended family would be together. This year we had to make an exception. My brother had children in elementary school, and November is prime flu and RSV season, so I looked at everyone like a walking petri dish. Due to Noah's extended hospital stay and compro-mised immune system, it was too easy for him to pick up a common cold and land back in the hospital. To prevent that from happening my brother and his family didn't spend Thanksgiving with us.

Navigating systems

Noah came home on a special formula that I was getting from our local health department via the WIC (women, infants, and children) program. Things were chaotic from visit one. They were adamant that Noah came with me so they could assess him before they could give him the formula. We went round after round about why I wouldn't bring him in—he just got out of the NICU where he spent five months; this was RSV season, and the WIC waiting room is full of petri dishes (kids 0-5 years old; several with coughs and snotty noses). The next issue of denying the formula in the same visit was because a piece of information wasn't filled in on their form. The information was on Noah's discharge papers which I provided but because it wasn't filled in by the physician before we left I needed to reschedule my appointment—that wasn't happening. We all had some choice words, yet I was finally able to get it resolved with the help of the nurse practitioner from the NICU. I had a very strained relationship with the dietitians that signed off receiving the special formula the entire time I participated in the WIC program.

It would be a great process improvement to allow children with compromised immune systems, who are seen on a regular basis by a handful of specialists to provide visit/follow-up notes and not be required to be assessed by a health department dietician or nurse.

Navigating my emotions

I did end up taking the antidepressants I received before

discharge, but I was inconsistent with them. I really struggled to be okay with taking them. I felt that I should be able to "overcome" and pray my way through. Prayer is important and effective, yet I now believe there are man-made helpers as well. A couple of years later I found a counselor/psychologist. I also really struggled with this decision, as I felt if I needed to see a counselor, then something was wrong with me and I was crazy. In reality, that's true, and it's not a bad thing. I had sustained major mental and emotional trauma with my birth experience, that doesn't even scratch the surface of all the other baggage that I had been carrying before Noah arrived. So yeah, something was wrong with me. I was a mess, and I needed to sort things out. I saw a counselor, off and on, for close to a year and during that time I would start and stop the antidepressants. I think I noticed the best results when I combined both treatments.

Today, I still deal with depression. It's not nearly as bad and I've been able to identify the source as situational or hormonal. I never did find myself being compliant with taking an antidepressant. I think a big part of it is because it's not an an immediate fix. It could take 4-6 weeks to see a difference, and honestly, I'm just not that patient. I have found yoga and meditation (I still pray), and that has been mind blowing in a great way. Yoga therapy (talk and movement therapy) is what really has enabled me to move through and process my feelings.

The unconventional way to find a pediatrician

We survived the weekend and now, Monday, we're off

to see our pediatrician. There was a big to-do about this before we left (who we were going to see), but we had it all straightened out by the time Noah was discharged. I arrived at the office, unloaded Noah and his equipment, checked us in, and learned that our pediatrician had a medical emergency and couldn't see us, but her partner would. I fill out the new patient paperwork and the clerk informed me we were still signed up under another pediatrician and had to be released from them in order to be seen.

I had no idea of who this other physician was that we were assigned to (Noah's insurance provider had just picked someone I guess). I had called to get switched, but they said I had to come in since Noah had never been seen there before. Thankfully, the other physician's office was less than five minutes from where we were. I arrive at their location, get Noah and his equipment out of the car. I get him checked in and tell them we need to be released from their care. I'm informed that he has to be seen and evaluated before he can be released. In my head, I'm thinking, "This is stupid, I'll just oblige and ask for them to see him." I'm then informed that they can't see him because they no longer accept his insurance. We then go round and round. If they can't see him, then they can't release him, but they won't because it's their policy to evaluate the patient before releasing them. I called the NICU office eliciting their help and followed their instructions to call the insurance company. The insurance company states they made the change. I go back to the pediatrician's office that we wanted to see, get Noah and his equipment out and check in. I'm told that they won't be able to see him because the partner with the medical emergency is going to be out for months, not a couple of days, as originally expected. SHIT, now what do I do?

I called the NICU office back to see if they could help me get in with the pediatrician we had discussed before Noah was discharged. I called the insurance company and got us switched, again. I called the potential new pediatrician's scheduling office and ran into brick walls at every turn. Their system didn't show that we selected them as a provider, they couldn't get him scheduled until that showed in their system, and they didn't have any appointments for a month. I'm a first-time mom, my child spent 153 days in the NICU, has a compromised immune system, is being primarily g-tube fed, has underdeveloped lungs, has to be given half a dozen medicines twice a day AND a diagnosis of failure to thrive, yet I'm supposed to wait a month before he's seen? Why is it okay to suggest this for my child, yet it's stressed and pressed upon parents of how imperative it is to see newborns 2-5 days after birth to ensure they're thriving, haven't lost a lot of weight, answer questions that the parents might have and so on?

To say I lost my shit is an understatement. I was so mad. I was at the end of my rope, so I thought. I cried a bit and then composed myself. I made sure my mom could watch Noah, and after dropping him off with her, I let out a primal scream in the car and drove down to the hospital. When I worked with the high-risk women and infants program I used to work with neonatologists and knew where their offices were. I made my way to their office, told the receptionist why I was there and sat on the floor behind the door until someone came and helped me get Noah an appointment that week with a pediatrician.

That was an unconventional move. The doctors weren't terribly happy I did that, but they helped me, and Noah was seen within two days. We've been with the same pediatrician ever since and wouldn't trade her for anyone else.

Life as a hermit

Because of the time of year and his ability to easily get sick, we became hermits with limited contact with the outside world. The most entertainment we had involved going to his pediatrician and specialist appointments each month. Occasionally, a friend would stop by, but due to my strict rules we didn't get, nor did I allow much company. If someone wanted to visit and they weren't coming straight from their house to mine, they had to bring a change of clothes. They had to change their clothes and wash their hands thoroughly before they could hold Noah. To keep from going completely stir crazy, we made trips to the park several times a week. Jenny and I would meet when we could to catch up and walk the kids a bit while working to get our bodies summer-ready. In May of 2010, Noah started attending "school." It was a day treatment center that only took care of medically fragile kids from birth to 5 years old. I didn't like the word "daycare," and I was sending him so he could learn—how to be around others, away from me, and taken care of by someone other than me, so I called it school.

June is our birthday month

June 2010 rolled around and it was time to party! We had a cookout at a local park with a Superman theme, as he truly was my Superman. Summers in Georgia are hawt so we had to wait for the sun to hide behind the trees before starting the festivities. By the time we got things going, Noah was asleep and slept through his party.

Noah had a challenging start, and I had a rude introduction to motherhood. We came, we saw and with determination and prayer learned to grow and conquer together.

Outro - Namaste on this roller coaster ride

Phew. Thank you for joining me on this roller coaster ride. The roller coaster of our life rolls on today.

Deciding to turn these candid journal pages into a book was both scary and exhilarating. Revisiting each journal entry eight years later was difficult. At times, I often felt like I was reliving the experience. I had to put this project down several times to compose myself. Even though reliving this journey was painful at times, it also reminded me to be grateful for the lessons I've learned and to celebrate just how far we've come.

If you're a parent who is in the NICU right now, consider this book a virtual hug. I am praying for your baby every day. If you're a medical professional, thank you for the work you do. I sincerely hope this book has helped you experience a different perspective.

Since Noah was deprived of oxygen before birth and sustained additional brain damage after birth due to a severe brain bleed. A diagnosis of cerebral palsy (CP) resulted. CP is one of the most common childhood disorders existing at birth that affects movement, muscle tone, and posture. There are different types and varying degrees; Noah is considered to have spastic quadriplegia, meaning he has a lot of stiffness (tone) and difficulty controlling the movements of his arms and legs. If you've been around him, you'll notice an arm will tend to "flail" or his movements seem irregular. It's hard for him to isolate specific muscles to make a movement happen, so when he wants to move, more muscles end up being activated than necessary. It's not impossible to isolate the muscles, just very, very difficult.

Today, Noah is visually impaired, and he uses a wheel-chair and assistive technology devices to communicate and play with some of his toys. Therapy, both physical and occupational as well as medication are the primary ways we work to overcome CP's effects. I've also introduced Noah to yoga which has done wonders for him by heightening his body awareness and untapped abilities.

Sometimes I hear people say someone, "suffers from cerebral palsy." Yes, this diagnosis comes with challenges. However, life isn't over; we go about our daily living, educational, and recreational activities in unconventional ways. For nearly every task, there's a way we can adapt it to accomplish our goals.

My ultimate goal is to help Noah achieve his highest level of independence, whatever that looks like for him. I hope as we're working towards our goal, we teach others along the way so they can see and unlock the potential for him and others who are differently-abled.

Noah is an active and funny boy who keeps me on my toes. To date, he has completed 3 triathlons, 5 marathons, and countless half-marathons and shorter distance races. I pushed Noah in his wheelchair for most of these, and we also have the help of our friends and running community to share in the fun of pushing. He attends school and has really come a long way. Like most grade schoolers, his favorite topic depends on the day, but he mostly enjoys his time interacting with his classroom friends.

Noah might be a train wreck on paper, and he still has a plethora of specialist and therapy appointments, yet he's so much more than the disabilities. He still has ups and downs, yet we live life to the fullest. We focus on his strengths while steadily working on the areas that we think can, and will improve. He laughs with his whole body, his smile lights up a room, he loves being read to, listening to music of all kinds, especially country, watching Wild Kratts, and painting. Noah is finding his voice and ability to express his likes and dislikes while exploring ways to gain independence.

God only gives you how much you can handle. I still think He overestimates my abilities at times, yet I'll continue to trust Him and make sure I'm buckled in for the remainder of our roller coaster ride.

Journey of faith

My faith and belief in Jesus Christ is what got and continues to get me through the good and especially the hard times. During Noah's time in the NICU, my faith and relationship with God was tested and ultimately renewed. I found myself more immersed in reading the Bible, pouring over scriptures, and reminding myself of God's promises. You can see and hear this throughout my journal entries in the book. Life after the NICU and even life today still bring many challenges and there have been times that I've been rocked to my core—emotionally, mentally, physically, and spiritually. True transparency, I've been mad with God. There have been times when I stopped talking to Him. The best advice I received was, "God is a big God. He can handle what you have to say, just talk to Him."
This topic could be a book in and of itself, and I plan to delve into this part of my life at a later time and in a different book. I want you to know, that because you pray and believe in God, that doesn't mean that you'll get the outcome that you hope for. The challenge, like in any relationship, is to maintain open and honest communication in the good times, and especially during the hard times.

Faith, just like life, is a journey not a destination.

Gratitude

Thank you for opening your heart and holding space for Noah and me.

Thank you, Muh, for all that you do. The notes, cards, words of encouragement, books, and prayers have helped more than you may ever know. Thanks for being my biggest and loudest cheerleader.

Pop Pop, you rock—we love and miss you. I'm thankful for the time that we had and the connection you and Noah were able to make. He will forever be your little "buddy."

I had every intention of publishing this book before my dad died. Suddenly and completely unexpectedly, he died just a few months before this book could come to life. He didn't know I'd turn these journal pages into a book, so this feels extra special to acknowledge him here. I know he is proud of me.

Jacq, thank you for being able to listen to and decipher my psychobabble and clean up my word vomit. It has truly been a pleasure working with you.

To the NICU staff (nurses, neonatologists, therapists, nurse practitioners, unit clerks, environmental services), THANK YOU! Thank you, for working in a world that many hear about yet few truly experience. Thank you for caring, loving, and praying for our kids. Thank you for standing in the gap for parents who can't be there. Thank you for trying and pulling out all the stops to give our kids a chance at life.

To Noah, thank you for teaching unconditional love—
not of you, but of myself. For helping me look outside
the box and how to fit a square peg in a round hole when
necessary.

To Charmane, for believing in me and the story that
I had was worth sharing. And for staying on me with
gentle reminders to complete this all the while helping
me bring it to fruition.

To Christina for your love, patience and artistic
ability to capture the full essence of Noah and I, from
the happy to extremely difficult times. Your heart bleeds
through your photography and is truly a gift never
to taken for granted.

To TieLeasha for jumping into this new world head
first and figuring it out with me. For giving me a sense
of normalcy, always being up for an adventure and
teaching your boys how different doesn't mean less.

To the strangers that I'll never meet in person yet you
prayed for Noah, and I through this whole journey,
Thank you.

To my church family for your prayers, love, support, encouraging words, faith, and willingness to learn and grow
in a different way.

To my family and friends for the ears that you lent,
shoulders for me to cry on, visits and opportunities for
respite, understanding when I was distant or curt, and
mostly just for loving us just the way we are.

I am beyond grateful to have you as a villager and a part of the Team Noah village. I offer you my deepest and sincere gratitude.

GO, NOAH GO!

"At times, our own light goes out and is rekindled by a spark from another person. Each of us has cause to think with deep gratitude of those who have lighted the flame within us." Albert Schweitzer

Resources

I am grateful to these organizations that helped make life in and out of the NICU a little better:

Websites and Support Groups

- Read more about Noah's adventures online at www.exceptionalliving101.org
- Caring Bridge - Where I originally shared each of these weekly entries. A personal health journal, rallying friends and family during any type of health journey. www.caringbridge.org
- Le Leche League USA - www.lllusa.org
- March of Dimes - www.marchofdimes.org
- Mocha Moms - www.mochamoms.org
- Parent to Parent USA - www.p2pusa.org
- Parent to Parent of Georgia - www.p2pga.org

Books
- Commanding Your Morning, Cindy Trimm
- Unlocking the Treasure: A Bible Study for Moms Entrusted with Special Needs Kids, Bev Roozeboom

If you're looking for reputable foundations to donate your time or resources, I suggest these:

- Kyle Pease Foundation - www.kylepeasefoundation.org/ support doesn't do research but is committed to individuals and families finding their place through sports
- UCP - United Cerebral Palsy www.ucp.org
- Your local children's hospital.

Glossary

Please keep in mind that I am not a medical professional and the words in this book are not medical advice. Here is a glossary containing explanations of the terms that may have left you scratching your head. These are here to make reading this book a little easier for you.

1. **APGAR** - a score given quickly to summarize a newborn's health and it stands for Appearance, Pulse, Grimace, Activity, and Respiration.
2. **Apneic episodes** - breathing stops for a period of time
3. **Aspiration** - when fluid or a foreign object goes into the airway—it can lead to pneumonia
4. **Barium** - a white compound used when conducting a swallow study using an x-ray machine
5. **Bradley method** - focuses on diet and exercise throughout the pregnancy and emphasizes that women should trust their body as childbirth is a natural process
6. **Brain regulation** - stabilization of fluid and blood flow through the brain and back out to the body
7. **C-Section** - cesarean section is a surgical incision to deliver a baby
8. **CO2** - carbon dioxide
9. **CPAP** - continuous positive airway pressure—provides mild pressure to keep the airway from collapsing
10. **CPT** - chest physical therapy—helps clear the airway using clapping (percussion)
11. **Cranial ultrasound** - picture of the brain produced by sound waves that's used primarily in infants due to their developing soft spots
12. **CT** - computerized tomography - provides a more detailed picture/image than regular x-rays
13. **De-sating episodes / desaturation episodes** - when oxygen levels drop drastically resulting in dramatic heart rate drops as well

14. **DNR** - do not resuscitate - an order that allows natural death and restricts CPR from being performed
15. **Echocardiogram** - ultrasound that uses sound waves to get pictures of the heart and its parts
16. **EEG** - electroencephalogram detects electrical activity in the brain
17. **EKG** - electrocardiogram checks the electrical activity of the heart
18. **EL** - elevated liver enzymes
19. **Enterococcus strain** - type of bacterial strain that causes infections
20. **Epi** - short for epinephrine—which is naturally found in our body as a hormone and plays a vital role in flight or flight response due to adrenaline. In this case, shots of epinephrine were given to stimulate the heart.
21. **Epilepsy** - chronic neurological disorder of seizures
22. **Episode** dramatic drop of heart rate and oxygen levels requiring intense medical intervention
23. **Fundoplication (Fundo)** - also called a Nissen - laparoscopic surgical technique to treat GERD - gastroesophageal reflux disease
24. **G-tube** - gastric feeding tube also called a "button" - inserted into the stomach and used to provide long-term nutrition for individuals who either can't eat or can't get all their nutrition by mouth.
25. **Gestational age** - weeks of pregnancy based on conception
26. **H1N1** - also known as Influenza Virus A, a subtype of the flu—the most common cause of the human flu pandemic in 2009 (https://medlineplus.gov/h1n1fluswineflu.html)
27. **HELLP** - a life threatening complication of pregnancy and is connected with preeclampsia. It stands for H-hemolysis, EL- elevated liver enzymes, LP- low platelet.
28. **Hydrocephalus** - also called "water on the brain" which means excessive fluid on the brain
29. **Incubator** - specialized medical bed for premature babies.
30. **IUGR** - intrauterine growth restriction

31. **IVH** - intraventricular hemorrhage also known as a brain bleed and graded 1 - 4; the higher the number, the more severe and likelihood of permanent brain damage
32. **LP** - low platelets
33. **MFM** - maternal fetal medicine specialist in high-risk obstetrics
34. **Micro preemie** - baby born under 800 grams or 1 ¾ pounds
35. **Milliliter (ml.)** - used to measure liquids. 10 ml. = 1 tsp.; 30ml = 1 tbsp. or 1 oz.
36. **Narcan** - reverses the effects of opioid medications
37. **Nasal cannula** - method used to deliver supplemental oxygen to a person that needs respiratory help; it's a flexible tube with two prongs that fit/sit at the nostrils' entrance
38. **NEC** - Necrotizing Enterocolitis - infection that affects and can ultimately kill a portion of the intestines; can be a life-threatening infection
39. **Neonatologist** - pediatric subspecialist that provides medical care for newborns, especially those that are ill or born prematurely
40. **Neuromuscular system** - includes all the muscles in the body and the nerves that make them work. All movement requires communication between the brain and muscles.
41. **NG** - nasogastric tube - plastic tube placed through the nose and ends in the stomach. Used to feed and give medicine to patients
42. **Nissen wrap** - also called a fundoplication - laparoscopic surgical technique to treat GERD - gastroesophageal reflux disease
43. **Occupational therapy** - assisting person to maintain or recover meaningful activities and abilities to do daily activities
44. **Oxygen saturation** - a way to determine oxygen-rich blood
45. **Paralytic** - medicine used to induce or cause temporary paralysis
46. **PDA** - patent ductus arteriosus - blood vessel that hasn't closed causing irregular blood flow between the heart and lungs

47. **Pediatric orthopedist** - physician specialist that evaluates and treats bones, muscles, and joints in children
48. **pH probe (test)** - test used to measure reflux (see GERD)
49. **PICC** - peripherally inserted central catheter. A thin, soft long (tube) allowing for long-term IV antibiotics, medications, and nutrition (TPN)
50. **Plastibell** - a form of circumcision
51. **Preeclampsia** - pregnancy complication usually associated when there's an increase in blood pressure
52. **PTSD** - post traumatic stress disorder
53. **Recathed** - recatheterization - this would have been done to collect additional urine sample
54. **Reflux** - stomach acid going back up to esophagus. Also see GERD.
55. **RSV** - Respiratory Syncytial Virus
56. **RT** - Respiratory Therapist - trained personnel that manages a patient's airway
57. **Seizure** - sudden and often uncontrolled electrical brain activity that affects how a person acts or feels
58. **Self-extubated** - deliberate removal of ventilator tube (breathing/respiratory support)
59. **Show out** - a "Naomi" term to describe when Noah would "act out" by dramatically dropping his heart rate and oxygen levels. Similar to him having a bad episode.
60. **SiPap machine** - respiratory support that gives patient a set number of "breaths" per minute
61. **Synagis** - a prescription medication typically given to infants at high-risk for severe lung disease if they contract RSV, a serious respiratory infection
62. **Umbilical hernia** - portion of the intestines push through a weak part of the abdomen causing a bulge in the belly button
63. **Uroseptic (Uroscpsis)** - severe and life threatening bacterial infection of the bloodstream and urinary tract
64. **Vagus nerve** - often called the cranial nerve. Runs from the head to the abdomen. Responsible for keeping a constant

heart rate and food digestion. When stimulated, it can cause a drop in blood pressure and heart rate.

65. **VCUG** - voiding cystourethrogram - special x-ray technique that looks at the urinary tract and bladder to see if urine is flowing the right direction

About the Author

Naomi Williams is a mother on a mission to help families and caregivers navigate life with differently-abled kids. She believes special needs kids, just like neuro-typical kids can and should lead an exceptional life.

She believes in celebrating individual abilities and that everyone is uniquely and wonderfully made. She wants to give everyone the opportunity to show off what they can do and not worry about being judged for what they can't. Naomi was born in Jeannette, PA and relocated with her family to Evans, GA. She's adapted to the southern way of life, yet she's a Yankee at heart. Naomi graduated from Augusta University with a Bachelor's in Health and Physical Education and became a Certified Health Education Specialist (CHES). She continued her education, and she now holds a Master's in Public Health from Walden University and is a Grief Support Specialist. Today, she works with families affected by cancer at a local hospital as a Family Support Coordinator. She also works as a trainer with an organization that provides resources for families raising individuals with special needs.

Educational and professional experiences have served Naomi well, yet it's her personal experiences that give her impressive credentials the street cred. She has always been passionate about empowering others to become their best, but it was the traumatic birth and the continued arduous responsibility of raising a medically involved and differently-abled child that fuels Naomi's passion for advocacy.

Naomi has been speaking to allied health, medical and nursing students, physicians, residents, educators, parents and community leaders about the connection and interdependence of raising a differently-abled child as a productive member of society. When she's not out there speaking to the community or medical professionals about the importance of advocacy and inspiring others to lead an extraordinary life, you'll probably find Naomi training for her next big triathlon or half-marathon, cheering Noah on in a marathon, roller skating, traveling and sightseeing, or taking a long deep breath on her yoga mat. You can learn more about Naomi on her website, www.naomidwilliams.com; and you can visit www.facebook.com/teamnoah09; where you can learn more about her son Noah and keep up with their shenanigans and misadventures.

Made in the USA
Columbia, SC
01 August 2020